Praise for Lane Denton
(from book signings, introductions, and political campaigns)

"History will record Lane Denton as the best legislator in history—and he was my friend."
–Jim Mattox, State Representative, Congressman, and recognized as the best Texas Attorney General in history

"...a friend and fellow fighter to keep the Big Boys honest."
–Jim Hightower, former Texas Agriculture Commissioner, author, and considered expert on food and nutrition

"To a friend, Lane Denton. Thanks for a good Democrat."
–Julian Bond, former Georgia State Senator, nationally recognized activist, and former President of the NAACP

"Lane Denton, Citizen Excelsior, in who faith and courage is vested in our future if we are to have one."
–Ronnie Dugger, Editor, *Texas Observer*, and author

"Lane Denton symbolizes something unfortunately unique in that he is a guy who really gives what you, the people, want and deserves...a chance at the dreams of the Founding Fathers."
–John Henry Faulk, nationally famous folk humorist, author, and stopped the black listing scandal in the 1950s Considered by many to be a hero and defender of the U.S. Constitution and Bill of Rights

"Lane Denton! Thanks for all you do."
–Dustin Lance Black, filmmaker, author, social activist known for writing the Academy-award-winning screenplay, *Milk*.

"To a long and very dear friend! I value our journey together! Much love, peace, and freedom!"
–David Mixner, civil rights activist and best-selling author, best known for his work in anti-war and gay rights. *Newsweek* named him The Most Powerful Gay Man In America.

"Denton, time and time again, has demonstrated his concern for the people of Texas."
–Editorial *Corpus Christi Caller-Times*

"He was bold, he was bright...Lane Denton played a crucial role in setting the pace and cutting the style for legislative reform."
–Harvey Katz, author of *Shadow on the Almo*, Doubleday

"Denton's record as a State Representative has been admirable and faithful to the interests of just folks, not special interests."
–John Moore, Editor, *The Marble Falls Highlander*

"...a damn good legislature when it comes to rolling up sleeves and showing some action in favor of the people."
–*The Hartford Brand*

"Denton is one of the solutions to our high utility prices."
–Bob Barton, Hays County Citizen

"To know Lane Denton is to believe in him, his capability, his integrity."
–*Waco Dispatch Press*

"You have always been a fighter, and I am honored to serve with you in the Texas Legislature."
–Dan Kubik, State Representative, and Chair, House Education Committee

"Lane, you had much to do with my decision to run. I figured that if we could get more 'Denton' types, we could easily make Texas a better place to live."
–Note to Lane Denton from Gonzalo Barrientos, longtime Texas State Senator

LANE & DENTON "The Dirty Thirty"

*The Real Texas Revolution:
An Inspiring Story of Thirty Courageous
Texas Legislators*

With
Frederick Williams

PAIREE PUBLICATIONS
San Antonio, Texas

Copyright © 2022 by Lane Denton.
All rights reserved.

No part of this publication may be reproduced, distributed, or transmitted in any form or by any means, including photocopying, recording, or other electronic or mechanical methods, without the prior written permission of the publisher, except in the case of brief quotations embodied in critical reviews and certain other noncommercial uses permitted by copyright law.

All photos used within are the property of the author.

Inquiries should be addressed to:
Pairee Publications
San Antonio, Texas
info@paireepublications.com
www.paireepublications.com

ISBN: 978-1-7371818-4-2

Editing, Cover, and Interior Design by:
Jessica Tilles/TWA Solutions.com

Printed in the United States of America

Distribution by
Ingram Content Group
www.ingramcontent.com

The dedication of this book is to all future leaders.

*My favorite future leader is my grandson, Denton Ryan Boatner.
Of course, he will make a great future governor of Texas.*

The Dirty Thirty

*A special dedication to thirty courageous legislators
who will go down in Texas history.*

Fred Anguish
Dave Allred
Maurice Angly,
Bill Bass
Tom Bass
John Bigham
Bill Blythe
Red Braun
Neil Caldwell
Tom Craddick
Lane Denton
Jim Earthman
Frances "Sissy" Farenthold
Bob Gammage
Ben Grant
Curtis Graves
John Hannah
Ed Harris
Fred Head
Zan Holmes
Edmond "Sonny" Jones
Walter Mengden
Tom Moore
Paul Moreno
Roy "Nick" Nichols
Charles Patterson
Dick Reed
Lindsey Rodriguez
Carlos Truan
Bob Vale

Acknowledgments

This book has been years in the making and its conclusion represents a lifelong love of politics. I will always be appreciative of my family and friends who have been loyal and dependable over the years. I will always be grateful to the thousands who helped in every one of my political campaigns. They are special and played a key role in my success. I had the outstanding assistance of Frederick Williams, who has a long history of teaching, community service, and is a nationally recognized author. I am appreciative of Jessica Tilles of TWA Solutions for the outstanding book cover and the interior text design that has made this book conveniently readable. My cousin, Linda Ables Kleiber ,wrote the book, *The Ables and Related Families*, which was an excellent reference. Thanks to G. Sterling Zinsmeyer, who made an excellent suggestion. Thanks to Guy Hundere for his excellent help!

Preface
by Frederick J. Williams

When I first met Lane Denton at a coffee shop across from San Antonio College, where I taught, he struck me as a rather gentlemanly, unassuming man with a great deal of intellect. We would meet and talk early in the morning before I went to my classes. Our discussions always covered what was happening in the political world—local, state, and national. At the time, I was writing an opinion column for the *San Antonio Express*, the only local newspaper in the city. As we got deeper into our discussions, I knew I was conversing with a man of tremendous depth.

After a few months of serious conversations, I shared with him that I had written a definitive history of Black Wall Street and the hate that destroyed it. He read my manuscript and volunteered to help with the book. He also suggested that I might be interested in writing about his life history. I asked him the usual question when someone tells me they want to tell their life story: "After family, who would be interested in reading about your life?" When he explained what he had accomplished as a state legislator in Texas from 1971 to 1977, I knew right away that my earlier assessment of him was correct. I jumped at the opportunity to work with him in getting his outstanding story out to the public.

Now, after several years of working on his life story, I am proud to announce that this is a book that thousands of men and women, who care about how government functions, to include the corrosive practices that make our democracy a mockery, should read.

One of the more intriguing aspects of his life story is how a young boy, born into a racist, very conservative state like Texas, could become a fighter for the underprivileged and why he, instead of going along to get along, took on the forces of power in the state and most times defeated them. This is sincerely a story of courage, commitment, sacrifice, and strength to fight and win. From the first week he stepped into the state legislature and took on the forces of power, including the Speaker of the House, he became the leader of a young, idealistic, and radical group of lawmakers dubbed the "Dirty Thirty." Normally that connotation would not have a positive meaning, but with Lane Denton and his entourage of fighters, it did. In this very compelling story of a man dedicated to changing our society through the legislative process, you will experience with him some battles he won and some he lost, but he always fought. That was and still is his nature.

Having taught Texas Government at the college level for years, I know what they put in the books to influence students to be good citizens. However, what they get is not what is really the truth. That is why Lane Denton's alternative presentation of just how the state government works should be a must-read for all our students, and that is why it is a must-read for all the citizens who care about our democracy.

In the Beginning

Lane Denton's first birthday.

Steve Martin, who was also born in Waco, Texas, in the same hospital, loved to tell the story of a newborn baby telling the doctor, "This is the best birthday I ever had."

For Tom and Fannie Denton, I was an unexpected present. I was the last of eight children, with five surviving. Their first three, born in the 1920s, did not survive.

Lane Denton

I could read before I started first grade. I had a unique advantage. My mother, Fannie Denton, taught first grade for thirty years. She was proud to tell everyone that every student always was a good reader. She was correct.

Regardless of their backgrounds, students hold one common factor: they must learn to read. Literature can change the world.

Lane, Fannie's star first-grade student.

Fannie Denton, a first-grade teacher for thirty years.

Lane Denton & "The Dirty Thirty"

President Lyndon Johnson was asked if anyone could understand what's it like to be President of the United States. He always told the story about his father, Sam Johnson, who served in the Texas House of Representatives. Representative Johnson said, "Son, you will never understand what it is to be a father until you are a father." I think the same can be said of every father and it also included the president. *Pictured: Lane, with his daughter, DeeAnn.*

Lane Denton

A classic one-building school, housing grades 1 through 12.

Lane Denton, Senior Class President and Student Body President

Joyce Argabright, Senior Class Secretary

Almost covered, right end of the top row. Coach C.C. Matthews, vocational agriculture teacher and scout leader. Take a look, you did exactly what he said.

High school basketball team—No. 80.

Letterman, co-captain
All Central Texas Team
Average 17 points per game.
Make a gallant, unsuccessful effort
for Baylor basketball team.

Lane Denton

Lane Denton, Center

AXTELL LONGHORNS

I was not happy, dressing in a boy scout/ military uniform. Twin brothers seemed ready to go.

The Axtell Boy Scouts

Lane Denton

The Axtell boy scouts helped people of Waco to recover from a 1953 tornado.

My brothers and sisters: Tom Denton, John E. Denton (twins), Dorothy Wood, and Sue Swaner.

Little league coach. Of course, we won every game.

Lane Denton

I always had major support from the working women and men.

Shelly, Kim, and DeeAnn were our essential assistants.

With my brother, Johnny, checking on his dairy farm.

Talking with DeeAnn and Shelly, Johnny and Charlene's daughter.

Steve Denton operates one of the best Grade A dairy farms in Texas. In case you are not aware, he gets up at 4:00 a.m. and completes his work at 10:00 p.m., seven days a week.

Announcing for State Representative. With a supporter like my daughter, DeeAnn, how could I lose? Almost one thousand supporters came to my announcement.

Introduction

Over my many years in politics and the positions I have taken, as you will read in this story of my life, many people have asked: How did a young boy, born and raised in conservative Texas, become such a progressive and liberal? Like everyone else, I am a product of the many experiences in my life. Not only was I born in a conservative but racially prejudiced part of Texas, I have fought to not be like the people in Waco who lynched and brutally killed a young Black man in 1917. My family, being from Falls County and with relatives in Waco, could not escape the story of James Washington. What made the Washington case historic was that a Waco photographer took pictures and the NAACP's *The Crisis* magazine covered the story. Beaton and dragged to the bridge over the Brazos River, a large crowd of over fifteen thousand people had gathered and watched as Washington was castrated, his fingers severed, and his body set on fire.

The events that impacted my life had a profound effect on my behavior as an elected state legislator, a candidate for the Texas Railroad Commission and Congress, even before I was born. The story was told to me that my maternal grandfather, Huson Ables, was a strong Democrat who hated Republicans, and the Republicans in the 1920s would have been Warren Harding, Calvin Coolidge, and Herbert Hoover. He blamed them for the economic troubles that had been plaguing the country. He and his brothers lost their Brazos Valley farms during the Republican years. In November 1929, he went out to help a neighbor get his car out of the mud. Very few roads, particularly in the rural areas, had gravel. Texas was one of the last states that did not have paved roads until the late 1940s, when the farm-to-market program led to the paving of roads in Texas.

My grandfather had hitched his horses up to the car and he was standing at the front. Something spooked the horses and pulled the car over him, crushing him. He lived for two weeks. His death was a real blow to my grandmother, his two daughters, and three sons. As a result of the accident, my grandmother had to sell the farm and move in with my parents. There were some advantages for my parents, Tom and Fannie Denton, with my grandmother living with them. She started getting a check in the late 1930s from the Texas Old Age Assistance Program. Her first check was for thirty-five dollars. My mother said it was a lifesaver for my grandmother from the Democratic Party. Hearing that story affected my thinking early on in life.

My paternal grandparents, Isaac Melton and Dora Ann Denton, also were farmers. They owned a farm in East Falls County. It was approximately two hundred acres and raised cotton, corn, fruits, and cattle. However, they both suffered from serious illnesses. My grandfather died from cancer in 1935, which forced my father and his five brothers to work on the farm. My grandmother suffered from a heart condition that took her life in 1938. She left the farm and one thousand dollars to each of her children, which in the late 1930s was a nice sum of money.

My interest in campaigns, elections, and politics began as early as 1949, when I was only eight years old. My sister was a candidate for Axtell School Carnival Queen and the way to win the contest was to sell chances on a particular item (I don't remember exactly what it was). I got four of my first-grade friends, Floyd Bradberry, Brenda

Bays, Woodrow Riley, and Martin Luther, to join me in convincing adults to buy chances to win the item. We made the most sales, she won, and that was my first victory. I was proud to see her in a brand-new red dress as the Carnival Queen.

In 1950, at age fifty-two, my father had his first severe stroke. It would take him over a year to recover. It happened in the fall and our cotton crop and other crops had to be harvested. Our neighbors came over and helped us with the harvest, and that had a lasting impression on me as to the goodness of people. It was an exceedingly difficult time for our family. My sister had to drop out of Southwest Teachers College. My father's medical bills were accumulating, and it would take years for us to pay them off. He was in Providence Hospital in Waco operated by the Sisters of Charity. This convinced me there was a need for national health insurance, which President Harry S. Truman advocated.

My two brothers and I had to work the one-hundred-twenty-five-acre farm, and we raised turkeys, chickens, pigs, and cattle. There were also fruit trees and a huge garden. We would go to the market on Saturdays and sell milk and eggs. After three years, my father was finally admitted to the University of Texas Medical Center in Galveston. There he was given an experimental drug that was a blood thinner. His health improved, but it was very difficult for him to do any kind of heavy work. His lifestyle as a farmer was limited, but he became an excellent supervisor.

In 1951, I experienced an illness that would have a direct effect on my thinking later in life. I came down with a severe ear infection that confined me to Providence Hospital for over a month. Three shots of penicillin every day finally broke the infection, and I recovered. My point here is that the lessons from my father's stroke and my illness drained our financial resources and we struggled to pay the doctors and the hospital bills. It is essential that we adopt a national health program for all our citizens. It is shameful that the United States is the only industrialized nation without comprehensive health care.

Lane Denton & "The Dirty Thirty"

It was the next year that my interest in politics bloomed. I listened to both the Democratic and Republican conventions on the radio because we did not own a television. I was eleven years old and my commitment to the Democratic Party was firm. I followed the nomination of Adlai Stevenson and was a firm supporter. My best friend, James Beaver, had an "Ike for President" button and I had an "Adlai for President" and we proudly displayed them. Having been a staunchly Democratic state for years, I just knew Texas would go to Stevenson, but Allan Shivers had become governor and, even though he was a Democrat, he pushed the voters to support Eisenhower. The key issue in Texas was over the Tidelands dispute. When oil was discovered off the coast of Texas, Shivers believed it should fall within the jurisdiction and control of the state. However, according to federal law, the state's jurisdiction ended at three miles. The oil was outside the three miles, so Shivers and his supporters made the argument the state jurisdiction should be three leagues, which would extend control to a little over ten miles. During the campaign, he asked each candidate if they would extend jurisdiction to the three leagues. Stevenson said, "No," and Eisenhower said, "Yes," and Shivers encouraged the voters to support the local and state Democratic candidates, but Eisenhower for president. It worked and a Republican carried the state for the first time since 1929. The Democrats lost that year because their candidate, Al Smith, was a Catholic. It was my first major disappointment, but it would not be my last. Stevenson was the better of the two candidates, and ten years later, President John F. Kennedy would appoint him ambassador to the United Nations.

By 1956, my interest had extended to state politics and national. At the state level, I became involved in the Tom Moore, Jr., for attorney general, George Nokes for lieutenant governor, and Ralph Yarborough for governor. I was also supporting Averill Harriman for president because Eleanor Roosevelt and Harry Truman had endorsed him over Stevenson. However, Stevenson won the nomination and chose a Southerner, Estes Kefauver, from Tennessee, for his running mate. All the candidates I supported lost. Eisenhower was easily reelected, and Yarborough lost in the primary by three thousand votes to Price Daniels, Sr., who had given up his senate seat to run for governor. Tom Moore, Jr., also lost in his race for attorney general. George Nokes also lost his race for lieutenant governor, and both the candidates were from Waco.

Elections have consequences. It is important to point out that if Yarborough had become governor and Moore, attorney general, Texas would be a quite different state today. This was my first experience and recognition of the power and control of the corporations and oil industry in Texas during this election. It would have made a big difference in the state to have had a solid progressive Democrat who cared about the people. Instead, we got elected officials who cared about protecting the interests of the rich and powerful.

My interest in politics was now quite strong. I worked in many of the local races in 1958 and even got Senator Ralph Yarborough's office to send me copies of the *Congressional Record* every day. I also followed politics in Washington, DC, with copies of *Time* and *Newsweek* that my aunt and uncle Elliott Ables provided to me. I also received my first lesson in dirty politics in 1956. Talking with the Yarborough people, they told me about an incident that occurred at Port Arthur in 1954. It had appeared that Yarborough might beat Shivers because of a major problem he had in the Veterans Land Insurance Industry. They needed to produce something that would turn the Texas voters against Yarborough. Then, only whites voted in the Texas Democratic primary.

The Shivers people borrowed several Cadillac cars from dealerships in Tyler and Longview, Texas. They placed Yarborough stickers on the bumpers and hired several Blacks to drive the cars, stopping at cafes and service stations and bragging that they were working for Yarborough. The white population was still angry about

Lane Denton & "The Dirty Thirty"

If you select the one hundred most important United States Senators, Ralph W. Yarborough would be at the top. Every major legislative action on civil rights, health care, environment, and education, he was the author.

I supported and worked in every campaign Senator Ralph W. Yarborough fought as the People's Senator." I was proud to help Senator Yarborough, especially since he was considered one of the best United States Senators in history. One of only three Southern Senators to oppose the "Southern Manifesto," which was opposed to racial integration in public places.

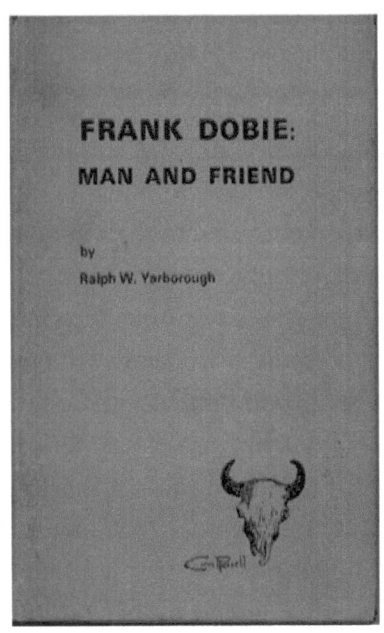

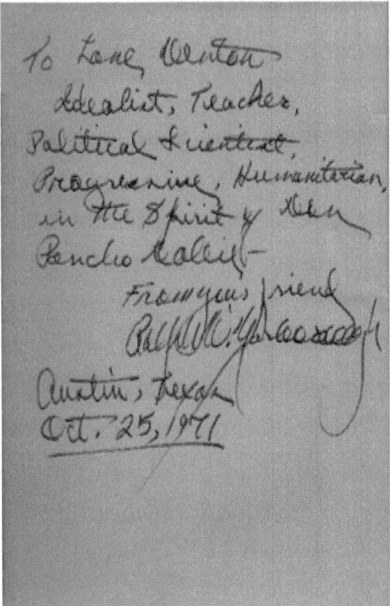

the May 1954 decision in the *Brown V. Board of Education* school desegregation decision. This short film, shown all over the state, just added fuel to the fire and the wrongs that Shivers had committed were soon forgotten. He was easily reelected governor.

Another incident that affected my thinking, socially and politically, was the polio epidemic that plagued our country. Every family worried that one of their children would be stricken with this devastating and crippling disease. I was fourteen and my twin brothers, Tommy and Johnny, were sixteen when Dr. Jonas Salk had discovered a safe vaccine to prevent the disease. My mother became incensed when it was announced nationally that the Republicans were delaying the distribution of the vaccine. FBI Director J. Edgar Hoover had sent a letter to President Eisenhower, warning that Salk's past political actions were far to the left. He stated that not only were the Salks liberals, but actually communists. Eisenhower responded, stating we needed to give the vaccine away even to the Soviet Union.

The stumbling block to getting the vaccine distributed was Health, Education and Welfare Secretary Oveta Cup Hobby from Texas. She was the wife of the former Texas Governor William Hobby and the owner of the *Houston Post*. She came to Washington and announced that she was there to bury the dream of socialized medicine. She believed the drug companies could move the vaccine to their regional distribution centers, and then to the doctors' offices and keep within the confines of the private sector. There was a nationwide outcry against her position. Editorials across the country wrote that she was incompetent, stupid, and heartless. Eisenhower finally came around and instructed the secretary to make it available to every American. It was told that Hobby put up one final fight in a cabinet meeting, arguing that it should not be given away free because that smacked of social medicine. Thanks to the president, she lost that argument, making it available nationwide and bringing an end to that dreadful disease. Before the vaccine, many people suffered. Polio struck one of my high school friends, Ginger Hawkins, and she was on crutches her entire life. State Representative Bobby Thomas, whom I replaced, gave up his seat in the legislature to run for county judge and was in a wheelchair because of the disease. Of course, we all are familiar with the plight of one of the most famous presidents, Franklin Delano Roosevelt, who suffered from polio and was on crutches and in a wheelchair throughout his long tenure as president.

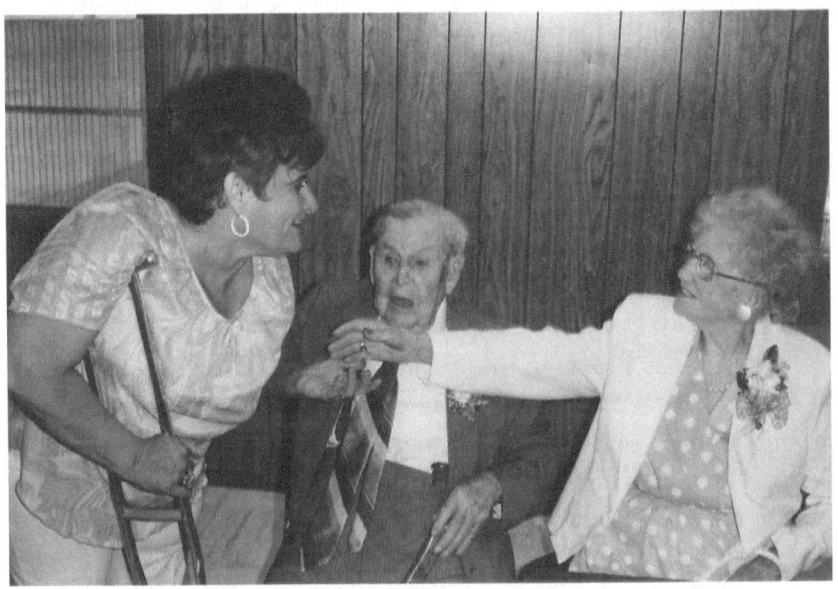

Ginger Hawkins (left, pictured with my parents), a classmate who developed polio, but always displayed courage.

Having graduated from Axtell High School in 1959, I entered Baylor University as a Political Science and Education major student. I immediately became continually active with the Baylor Young Democrats. Price Daniels, Jr., son of the man who had beaten Yarborough for governor in 1956, and the man who would eventually

Lane Denton

Baylor University graduation picture.

I had no idea in 1957 when I looked up at the sky, trying to locate the Soviet Sputnik, that it would be my ticket to attend college. I was busy communicating with my congressman, W.R. Poage, for an appointment to West Point. Unsuccessful, I entered Baylor University with a National Defense Education loan Congress had passed after the Soviet Sputnik.

I entered Baylor University in the summer of 1959, and my first class was in Pat Neff Hall. I received my Bachelor of Science in 1962. My post-graduate work was at the University of Texas and I attended law school.

After my race for State Treasurer, I decided to spend time as a law student at Thurgood Marshall School of Law, Texas Southern University.

Dr. Thomas Freeman insisted that the next direction for me would be a legal first for justice and equality. Dr. Freeman was an outstanding teacher, having taught both Barbara Jordan and Martin Luther King, Jr. His debate team in 1956 defeated the debate team from Harvard.

Another outstanding professor was Earl Carl. Professor Carl, even though he was blind, was one of the most outstanding torts professors in the United States.

Pat Neff Hall, named for Governor of Texas and President of Baylor University.

Lane Denton

DUPLICATE

Denton, Kenneth L.
_____Name_____ $ 5,000.00
                            Amount

BAYLOR UNIVERSITY
WACO, TEXAS

                    June   18   19 59
                    ____Date____

PROMISSORY NOTE

I, Kenneth L. Denton_____, hereinafter called the maker, promise to pay to BAYLOR UNIVERSITY, hereinafter called the Institution, located at Waco, Texas, the sum of $ 5,000.00 or so much thereof as may from time to time be advanced to me and endorsed hereon together with all attorneys' fees and other costs and charges for the collection of any amount not paid when due according to the terms of this note.

The maker further understands and agrees, and it is understood between the parties that:

I. Repayment of such principal, together with accrued interest thereon at the rate of 3 per centum per annum computed from the date of the first required payment, shall be made in 10 equal annual installments, unless prior to the maker's ceasing to be a full-time student at the above named institution the maker has elected to repay such principal, together with accrued interest thereon at the rate of 3 percentum per annum computed from the date of the first required payment in accordance with the terms of a graduated schedule approved by the above named institution and the Commissioner of Education of the United States, hereinafter called the Commissioner, which schedule when agreed upon shall be attached to and become a part of this note. In either case the maker shall commence repayment (except when Paragraph IV(3) applies) of the principal that appears on the face of this note and accrued interest not later than one year after the date of ceasing to be such a full-time student in an institution of higher education as defined in the National Defense Education Act of 1958 and Federal Regulations pertaining thereto.

II. Any interest not paid on the principal as it becomes due shall be added to the principal and become a part thereof, and thereafter bear interest at the same rate as the principal.

III. All sums advanced pursuant to this note are drawn from a fund created under the National Defense Education Act of 1958. Such terms of this note as are subject to interpretation shall be construed in the light of regulations of the Commissioner, a copy of which shall be kept by the institution.

IV. This note is subject also to the following conditions:

  (1) No monies shall be advanced to the maker unless he (a) has executed and caused to be filed with the Commissioner an affidavit that he does not believe in, and is not a member or supporter of any organization that believes in or teaches the overthrow of the United States Government by force or violence, (b) has subscribed to an oath or affirmation of allegiance to the United States and of willingness to defend the Constitution against all its enemies, and (c) is a full-time student maintaining satisfactory standing at the above named institution.

  (2) The maker may at his option and without penalty prepay all or any part of the principal and accrued interest at any time.

  (3) Interest shall not accrue on the loan, and periodic installments need not be paid, during any period (a) during which the maker is pursuing a full-time course of study in an institution of higher education, or (b) not in excess of 3 years during which the maker is a member of the Armed Forces of the United States; any such period in (a) or (b) shall not be included in determining the ten-year period during which repayment must be completed.

  (4) If the maker undertakes service as a full-time teacher in a public elementary or secondary school (in a State or in Hawaii, Puerto Rico, the District of Columbia, Canal Zone, Guam, or the Virgin Islands), the amount of this note shall be reduced at the rate of 10 percentum of such amount

Lane Denton & "The Dirty Thirty"

    plus interest thereon, which was unpaid on the first day of such service, for each complete academic year of such service, up to a maximum of 50 percentum of the principal plus interest thereon.

    (5) In the event of the maker's total and permanent disability or death, the unpaid indebtedness hereunder shall be cancelled.

    V. The maker shall certify that he has received no other National Defense Student Loan except as indicated in the Schedule of Previous National Defense Student Loans below:

Date 6-18-59   Signed Kenneth Lane

Caveat — This note shall be executed without security and without endorsement, except that, if the maker is a minor and this note would not, under State law, create a binding obligation, either security or endorsement may be required.

Co-Signer J. T. Denton

SCHEDULE OF PREVIOUS NATIONAL DEFENSE STUDENT LOANS

	Amount	Date	Institution	Signature
1	$			
2				
3				
4				

SCHEDULE OF ADVANCES

	Amount	Date	Signature
1	$ 150.00	6-18-59	Kenneth Lane Den
2	150.00	8-17-59	Kenneth Lane Dent
3	300.00	9-14-59	Kenneth Lane Den
4	300.00	1-13-60	Kenneth Lane Dent
5	100.00	6-8-60	Kenneth Lane Dent
6	300.00	9-20-60	Kenneth Lane Dent
7	300.00	2-1-61	Kenneth Lane Dent
8	350.00	9-12-61	Kenneth Lane Dent
9	350.00	1-30-62	Kenneth Lane Dent
10			

PAYMENTS ON NATIONAL DEFENSE STUDENT LOAN

Date	Amount of Payment		Interest	Received by
	Total	Principal		
	$	$	$	

Lane Denton

BAYLOR UNIVERSITY
Office of the Dean of Instruction
WACO, TEXAS 76703

GEORGE M. SMITH
Dean

October 14, 1964

Mr. Kenneth Lane Denton
1200 Lewis
Waco, Texas

Dear Mr. Denton:

You will be pleased to know that you are on the Dean's Distinguished Honor List for the Summer Session, 1964. You made a grade average of 3.80 or better for the semester while taking not less than 12 semester hours. You are one of 22 students, 10 men and 12 women, attaining this distinction. Also, you will be glad to know that you are one of 19 students making "A" in all subjects in the Summer Session.

I am sure that you feel a justifiable pride in your achievements here. We hope that you will continue to do as well.

Sincerely yours,

George M. Smith
Dean of Instruction

GMS:pag

Lane Denton & "The Dirty Thirty"

BAYLOR UNIVERSITY
Office of the Dean of Instruction
WACO, TEXAS

GEORGE M. SMITH
Dean

July 2, 1962

Mr. Kenneth Lane Denton
Route 1
Axtell, Texas

Dear Mr. Denton:

You will be pleased to know that you are on the Dean's Honor List for the Spring Semester 1962. You made a grade average of at least 3.60 but less than 3.80 for the semester while taking not less than 15 semester hours. You are one of 91 students, 44 men and 47 women, attaining this distinction.

I am sure that you feel a justifiable pride in your achievements here. We hope that you will continue to do as well.

Sincerely yours,

George M. Smith

George M. Smith
Dean of Instruction

GMS:bmb

become Speaker of the House of Representatives, was also a member. We both worked on the Kennedy/Johnson campaign for president as youth coordinators for central Texas. In that capacity, I became very close to Sam Rayburn, Speaker of the United States House of Representatives. He made numerous trips to Waco and always stayed at the Roosevelt Hotel. I ran errands for him, like buying cigarettes. He was a chain smoker. He also liked whiskey, but I was too young to bring that to him. He smoked unfiltered Camel cigarettes, and they ultimately led to his cancer that took his life in November 1961, right after Kennedy was elected president. He did everything to convince me to be his assistant in Washington, DC, but I had just finished my first year at Baylor, so there was no way I could accept his offer. Rayburn taught a lesson that would remain with me throughout my political career. He told me that his district comprised small towns and did not have one single Chamber of Commerce in them. I think if you analyze that all over the country, the Chamber of Commerce is anti-union, anti-workers, and against doing anything that is beneficial to workers, everyday citizens, and the elderly. They have a network in every larger city, and they are highly effective all over Texas. I learned that the hard way in my run for railroad commissioner and for Congress years later.

 I was at the Roosevelt Hotel the night that former President Harry Truman came to Waco from San Antonio where he had made the statement, "Any Democrat that votes for a Republican should go straight to hell." That caused quite a stir in the hotel. Otis Gardner, Tom Moore, Jr., and Chloe Armstrong were there and concerned that he might repeat those same words that night. They decided the only person who could talk the former president into not repeating that same statement was his wife, Bess Truman. They got her on the phone, put her on hold, and they gave the phone to Truman as soon as he walked into the room. She convinced him not to repeat those lines, and he delivered an outstanding speech that night before a large crowd at the Heart of Texas Coliseum.

Lane Denton & "The Dirty Thirty"

During the 1960 campaign, I learned that you had to have some dependable supporters you could trust and, at other times, had to use the stick instead of the carrot to get what you needed. In the fall of that year, I accompanied Otis Gardner to the Kyle Hotel in Temple, Texas. We were attending a secret meeting with Robert Kennedy, who flew to meet with many of the bankers and members of the Chamber of Commerce. Kennedy was not in a good mood because he felt they were not supporting his brother as he felt they should. Word had reached the campaign headquarters that several Chamber members and bankers were going to support Nixon. He read them the riot act. "If you don't get the vote out for John Kennedy," he said, "you can count on no support and no federal financing for Texas." The Kennedy/Johnson ticket carried Texas that year by only forty-six thousand votes and had a lot to do with their winning the election. I met the president twice during the campaign, but I was not as lucky as another young volunteer, Bill Clinton. He had a picture taken with the president when he attended the Boys State Conference at the White House. President Clinton always said that photo was the most prized possession he had. He used it a great deal in his 1992 presidential campaign and earlier campaigns, some he won, and having lost a race for Congress.

The era of the 1960s was dominated by Black Americans fight for equal justice in their country. It had a tremendous impact on my outlook on life and was one of the main reasons I would jettison the attitudes of many in my community. It all began with the murder of young Emmett Till in 1955. Like most other caring people, I was moved when I saw the picture of Till in his casket, face blown up so that you could not recognize him. It was a brave decision that his mother, Mamie Till, made when she had an open casket, stating that she wanted the "entire world to see what they had done to her son." Emmitt was my age, and I felt the pain that his mother shared with the world.

When we would go into Waco on Saturdays, I would stare at the signs reading "Colored Water Fountain" and "White Water Fountain." I thought how ridiculous. Then to go into Woolworths, Sears, and Montgomery Wards and know that Blacks could not eat at the lunch counter, as well as separate restrooms, just seemed senseless. I just could not believe nor accept the ignorance of people who would take water hoses and turn them on women and children who wanted nothing more than to be treated as equals. Watching this abuse to other human beings and, more important, American citizens had a profound effect on my attitude, behavior, and actions once I was elected to the Texas State Legislature. In the fall of 1961, I observed that hatred up close.

I was dating Betty Kirbo, who would later become my wife. She was a reporter for UPI and KWTX Television and was assigned to cover a 1961 Ku Klux Klan rally in Groesbeck, Texas. I drove her there, and it was a troubling event to cover. I saw the hatred that individuals can have. At the conclusion of the rally, dressed in their white robes and faces covered with a mask, they all marched around a cross that was ablaze. What was most amazing was that they all were carrying Bibles.

Another incident in 1963 that had a profound impact on what would be my future in politics occurred when Vice President Lyndon B. Johnson visited Dallas. The arch-conservative billionaire Texas oilman, H. L. Hunt, and his "Lifeline and Facts Forum" blasted the airwaves daily, stirring up hate among the people of Texas. His national program talked about the evils in America and part of that evil was the Kennedy administration. When Johnson made his way into the Baker Hotel, a mob from Highland Park confronted him, shouting hateful epithets and spitting at him, which was led by right-wing Republican Congressman Bruce Aleger. Years later, Stanley Marcus, who was there with the vice president and Lady Bird Johnson, told me it was the scariest event of his life. They barely escaped from the Baker Hotel to the Adolphus Hotel.

Lane Denton & "The Dirty Thirty"

On November 22, after a morning rally in Fort Worth, Texas, President Kennedy and Jackie landed at Love Field in Dallas. Adlai Stevenson had warned him that hatred for him and the liberal establishment was so intense that he should cancel his trip. When he disembarked the plane, he was handed a copy of the *Dallas Morning News*, opened to the following political advertisement:

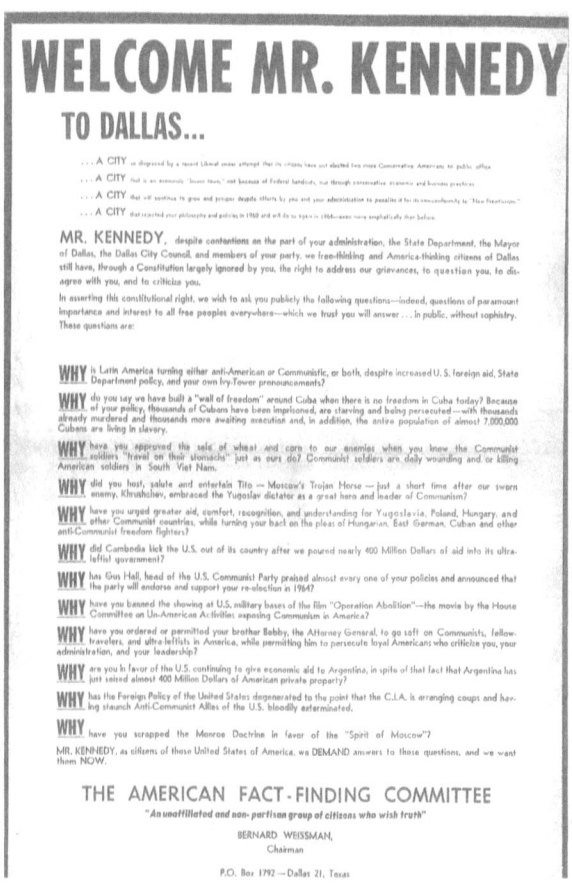

This is the full-page ad that greeted President Kennedy when he arrived in Dallas. This is an example of the far-right hate that occurred in America in 1963.

Instead of taking Stevenson's advice, supported by this ad in the newspaper, he simply tossed it aside and told Jackie, "We have now entered nut country." That same morning, it was "nut country" that assassinated him.

By 1967, I knew my future lay in politics within the Democratic Party. I also knew I would not be an established and controlled Democrat. I was bent on breaking the hold that men like Shivers and Connally had over the party and doing away with the corruption that ran rampant throughout the halls of the state legislature and in the governor's office. I was not yet sure when I would run for office, but that was my future. That same year, I went with my friend, Otis Gardner, to hear Vice President Hubert Humphrey speak at the Adolphus Hotel in Dallas. I had an opportunity to visit with the vice president. In his speech that night, he shared with us in the audience the fact that 100% of the Republicans serving on the House Committee in 1935 voted against the Social Security legislation and 85% when it reached the House of Representatives floor for a final vote. Thirty years later, 90% of Republicans voted against the Civil Rights Bill, the Voting Rights Bill, and the Elementary and Secondary Education Bill.

My second love, besides politics, was education. After graduating from Baylor University with a degree in Education and a minor in Political Science in June 1962, I took a job teaching at Mart Independent School District in the eastern part of McLennan County. Mart only had one school then, and it encompassed grades 1 through 12. I taught a variety of classes at different grade levels. I taught American History to juniors in high school and science to sixth-graders, and finally a class on health to fourth and fifth-grade students. For the one year I was at Mart, I was the assistant coach on the high school football team, head baseball coach, and as well as the junior high school boys' basketball team. The school was still

Lane Denton & "The Dirty Thirty"

S. SENATOR... **JOHN F. KENNEDY** FOR PRESIDENT
★ ★ ★ ★

HEADQUARTERS · 1106 CONNECTICUT AVE., N.W. · WASHINGTON, D. C. · DISTRICT

My Dear Fellow Campaign Workers:

  Both Senator Johnson and I are exceedingly grateful to you and your fellow students who are giving so generously of your time and effort on our behalf. One of the great things about this campaign has been the warmth and response shown us by the young men and women in our colleges and universities.

  This campaign is going to be very hard fought, and very closely decided. The efforts which you make on our behalf both on and off the campus will have a very direct bearing on the outcome.

  I believe that the challenge of our New Frontier program is one which will evoke a strong response from those who care about tomorrow. I know that those ideas are worth every bit of effort which the struggle to obtain them will demand.

  I am happy to see that in such a contest, you have chosen to take your place in the front lines among those who want to see our nation live up, in every way, to the great potential which we know is ours.

  Senator Johnson and I will do everything to be fully worthy of your confidence, just as our confidence in your devotion and ability to get the job done makes us very proud to be associated with you at one of the crossroads of history.

Sincerely yours,

John F. Kennedy

OFFICIAL CAMPAIGN MANUAL

Personal Copy of Lane Denton

Students for Kennedy · Johnson

GUIDE TO VICTORY

Lane Denton

Lane Denton & "The Dirty Thirty"

President John F. Kennedy came to Texas to help mend the rift between Governor John B. Connally and Senator Ralph Yarborough. The final event was to be a unity dinner in Austin. To note, Senator Yarborough was left off of the program. The conservative Texas establishment did not help mend the rift.

segregated despite the *Brown v. Board of Education* Supreme Court school desegregation decision in May 1954. Segregation still ruled the day in Texas.

After that one year at Mart, I moved on to Connally High School and Junior High School, both next to Connally Air Force Base. Because many of the students came from military families, both schools were integrated, something that did not exist in other schools in the Waco community. As a result of that experience, it became quite clear to me just how important it was for all the schools to integrate. The exchange of views on life that different racial groups have in the classroom influences ideas and perspectives on race among the young. The biases and prejudices they received at home were countered by the very experiences the children had as they intermingled with different groups. Those two years would affect my behavior once I entered the political arena as an elected official eight years later.

Approximately half of my students at that school were sons and daughters of high-ranking military personnel. One student, Lucius Clay III, was the grandson of a famous general, Lucius Clay, who was in control of the reorganization of Berlin after the Germans surrendered in 1945. His father was the head of the Twelfth Air Force Battalion, a major position of responsibility. Working with the parents of my students had given me the unique opportunity to better understand world affairs.

On November 22 of that year, the entire country was shocked and thrown into a terrible whirlpool of sadness as President Kennedy was assassinated, only one hundred miles from our school, in Dallas, Texas. The day before the assassination, my lesson with my government class dealt with the succession to the presidency if something happened to the president, according to the United States Constitution. Kenneth Woods, a young Black student in the class, was to prepare a paper on the succession for the next day.

Kennedy was scheduled to talk in Dallas and that night attend an event in Austin. Otis Gardner had purchased tickets to the event through Senator Ralph Yarborough. It was to be a special banquet for the president, and I was overjoyed at the possibility of being in the same room at the Austin Municipal Auditorium with the president. Otis, one of the state's leading Democrats, explained to me that the reason for Kennedy's visit to Texas was to patch up problems within the state between John Connally's very conservative faction and the liberal faction controlled by Senator Yarborough. Connally knew the Republicans would not bother to field a candidate in the 1964 senatorial race. He wanted to beat Yarborough in the primary with a much more conservative candidate. They floated the rumor that Congressman Jim Wright from Fort Worth would run against Yarborough.

It complicated the situation even more with the battle between Vice President Lyndon Johnson and Senator Yarborough on federal judgeship appointments. Yarborough felt he should take the lead in the appointment process. Johnson wanted to be the go-to guy for Texas. With the assistance of Speaker of the House Sam Rayburn, Yarborough got two outstanding judgeship appointments nominated by the president and approved in the Senate. One of those appointees was Judge William Wayne Justice from East Texas, who became one of the most courageous federal judges in the history of the country. The other was Judge Sarah Hughes, who was a close friend of Speaker Rayburn. An outstanding Democrat, I met Judge Hughes three times. She was a dynamic woman, all five feet one and one-half inches of her. She served three terms in the House of Representatives. She was the first woman appointed as a state district judge by Governor James Allred. She had known Speaker Rayburn for an exceptionally long time. In fact, Attorney General Bobby Kennedy felt she was too old and did not want her name sent to the Senate for confirmation. However, Speaker Rayburn, in his typical fashion, quietly told Bobby Kennedy that there would be no funding for the Department of Justice until she was nominated and confirmed. He won out and

Hughes became the judge who swore in Johnson on Air Force One after President Kennedy died in Parkland Hospital.

The morning of November 22, I was ecstatic at the plans for that evening. However, at 12:30 p.m., the principal announced over the loudspeaker that "President John F. Kennedy had died at 12:30 p.m." The entire school and my classes were thrown into shock. Kenneth Woods never got a chance to make his report. The entire country was in mourning for quite a while, and that included me.

As a career move in 1965, I accepted a position at University Junior High School in Waco. I accepted the position and, in doing so, I returned to the segregated school system. Returning to segregated schools after experiencing the value of integration, I was determined to bring about change in the Waco School District. I sought allies to assist me in this mission. It would be a valuable learning experience that I would utilize later in my years in the state legislature.

The first person I met was Dr. Priscilla Meyers, a very active member of the American Government Employees Association in Waco. She was a liberal and very much committed to integrating public schools. She was also friendly with several influential Blacks in the Waco community and introduced me to Reverend Robert Gilbert, a Black activist, Ulysses Cosby, and Cullen Harris, all leaders who would be helpful in the attempt to integrate the schools.

In the summer of 1967, assistant superintendent of the Waco School District, Dr. Barry Thompson, offered me the position of assistant principal at North Junior High School. This promotion offered me an opportunity to collect statistics as proof of deliberate segregation at University Junior High and North Junior High. My intent was to get the numbers to the local president of the National Association for the Advancement of Colored People (NAACP) to be used in a potential legal suit. I had several confidential meetings with Dr. Priscilla Meyers, along with Dr. Vivian Malone-Mays, the wife of a local dentist, and her mother, Mrs. Malone, who was regularly active in the local chapter of the NAACP. An attorney from Little Rock, Arkansas, who was interested in our findings, came to Waco and discussed how we should proceed against the Waco School District. We had built up a very persuasive case against the Waco Independent School District, and later they negotiated an out-of-court agreement to integrate all the schools.

In December 1967, I had my first opportunity to test the waters of the political world and how I might fit into it. Governor Connally appointed State Representative George Cowan chair of the State Board of Insurance. That left the seat representing Waco and surrounding areas vacant. It fell within my jurisdiction. I ran for the office but could only campaign during the Christmas holiday. Once the holiday was over and I assumed my duties with the school system, my time to campaign was limited. I did quite well, finishing third among a slate of seven candidates, and I only spent three hundred dollars. Tom Moore, Jr., won the election, which did not sit well with the power brokers in the district. He was too much of a progressive liberal for them. It was also a sign that the political climate in the Waco area was changing.

My final promotion and last job within the Waco School District came early in 1968. Dr. Barry Thompson asked me to take over the position of director of Visiting Teachers Services in the Waco Independent School District. I assumed responsibility for fifteen thousand students labeled as troubled, with unique learning problems, failing in school, and living in dysfunctional homes. I had a great staff led by Walter Napier, a two-hundred-fifty-pound former Dallas Texan football player, my assistant. Otto Deutchman served as my main coordinator receptionist. Maxine Flynn and Anne Prestige were my other assistants. Under my leadership, the entire team worked to make sure there were no dropouts and to get students into special summer programs. We also set up a special sports program, and I insisted it be integrated. We began a special school for pregnant young girls, the first in the Waco School District. Before our program, pregnant students were arbitrarily dismissed from school.

We made special appeals to the Kiwanis Club, the Lions Club, the Rotary Club, the Salvation Army, and Goodwill for donations of clothes for our needy students. We also arranged for the students to get dental care, eyeglasses, and set up a free lunch program for them.

During that year, I received an unexpected telephone call from Robert Choate, an independent Washington, DC, consumer advocate, who was doing nutrition research. He explained that legislation to expand the school lunch program had been bottled up in the Agriculture Committee in the House of Representatives. The chair of the committee was W. R. (Bob) Poage from Waco. A report had circulated that serious malnutrition was occurring in Poage's district, Falls County, which was predominantly Black.

I went to Falls County, one of the poorest counties in the nation, with a family income average of $2,287 a year, and worked with James Lynn, president of the local branch of the NAACP. We documented and obtained statements from the residence as to the extent of the malnutrition and the need for the lunch program to counter that problem. The community was over 50% African American and many of the people had come there without jobs or financial means to survive. This naturally affected their children. They needed free lunch in order to function at school. James Lynn took photographs of the practically starving children and attached them to the report I sent to Senator Ted Kennedy. Our research served as a catalyst for Choate to put pressure on Poage to approve the legislation, which he finally did in 1969. I consider this one of my major achievements, because I believe school breakfast and lunch should be free in every public school in the country.

My interest in politics continued to grow when I was asked to be the Democratic Precinct Chair of Bellmead, the largest precinct in McLennan County. It was listed as Box 17 and was called Lavega. It was also the largest voting box in McLennan County. As the precinct chair, it allowed me to know every Democratic Precinct Chair in McLennan County and added to my list of names of the important Democrats I needed to know for the future.

As a result of my position as the precinct chair, I automatically served as the election judge for the polling site, Box 17, on election day in November 1968. I oversaw hiring all the workers for that particular voting poll. I was also responsible for hiring the deputy election judge. On election day, I greeted all the voters and answered questions they might have had. I met every single person who voted in that precinct that year. It gave me a considerable advantage as I considered a possible run for state legislature in 1970.

Finally, in December 1969, I decided to make a run for the Texas State Legislature. The two seats in the legislature allotted to McLennan County appeared on the ballot as Place 1 and Place 2. Tom Moore represented Place 1 and fortunately, it was not the seat that I had sought. Place 2 was filled by Bobby Thomas. But he gave up his seat in the state legislature and ran for County Judge. That opened up his seat, and I jumped on the opportunity when I first got word that he had vacated that seat.

The word throughout the district was that Mickey Holmes, assistant to Poage, was a shoo-in to win. Local businesses, the Chamber of Commerce, the daily newspapers, and, of course, the congressman supported him. They gave me no chance of winning at all. However, my roots were firmly planted in the county. I had great support from the families of the students at the schools where I taught. I had extraordinarily strong support from the Black community since I had, over the years, established a reputation for being passionately committed to fighting for their causes. With tremendous assistance from my family, I took on the challenge with great alacrity. I better understood the needs of the people in the district since I had lived with them all my life. We sent out over ten thousand letters to constituents in the district, clearly identifying the issues most important to them. I must have shaken every hand with all the men and women, as well as their children, in the district.

Against all the odds, I won the Democratic nomination and the general election. Taking on the odds would define my career in politics. At twenty-nine years old, I was now a member of the Texas State Legislature and would embrace the role of representing the underrepresented to include all minority groups and the poor, not only in my legislative district but throughout the entire state.

Staff of Waco ISD's Visiting Teacher's Service. This group worked seven-day workweeks. Their responsibilities included working with learning challenges, school lunch, drop-outs, truants, pregnancy, juvenile court cases, suicide prevention. Every school should have a similar staff.

Lane Denton & "The Dirty Thirty"

I always remember the words of Booker T. Washington: "The highest test of civilization of a race is its willingness to extend a helping hand to the lest fortunate." As Director of Visiting Teacher Service, I made it a point to visit classrooms as often as I could and knew the children's names.

Otto provided me with an important education: movie theaters could refuse to sell tickets to wheelchair users, with little support for the blind and deaf. When I entered the legislature, the vast majority of children with disabilities were institutionalized, and most denied education.

I urged successfully for President Carter to include disabilities under the Rehabilitation Act of 1973. The efforts would continue until the passage of the American Disabilities Act of 1990.

My assistant, Otto Deutchman, coordinated our schedule, answered phones, and was essential in making our staff work.

Opening Day—January 12, 1971

Lane Denton & "The Dirty Thirty"

When I walked on the floor of the Texas House of Representatives on January 12, 1971, to be sworn in as a freshman legislator, the issues in Texas were urgent.
- Impossible to obtain public records.
- Blatant corruption.
- Secret meetings and votes at local, state agencies.
- Almost no meaningful financial disclosures for public officials.
- State budget written in secret.
- School finance system ruled unconstitutional.
- Warehousing mentally and physically challenged individuals.
- Prison system in need of major reform.
- Seniors voiced discrimination in state employment.

As I looked at this tiny machine on each member's desk, I realized its importance in determining the future of our state. I considered every vote an awesome responsibility. For me, voting "present" was not an option—I never did.

Talking with Betty on opening day about how Speaker of the House runs the House of Representatives with total control. She would later see for herself, serving nine terms in the House.

The night before opening day, a gala celebration was held to introduce new members.

Lane Denton & "The Dirty Thirty"

DEMOCRATIC VICTORY DINNER

January 18, 1971, Municipal Auditorium, Austin, Texas

PROGRAM

Master of Ceremonies
  Elmer C. Baum, Chairman, State Democratic Executive Committee
Music
  Longhorn Band, Wind Ensemble Volunteers, conducted by Vincent R. Di Nino
Entrance of National and State Officials at Head Table
Invocation
  Dr. Guy Newman, President, Howard Payne College, Brownwood
National Anthem
Recognition of Members, State Democratic Executive Committee
Introduction of the Honorable Gus F. Mutscher, Speaker of the House of Representatives
Introduction of the Democratic Members of the Texas House of Representatives
Introduction of Senator Jack Hightower, President Pro Tempore of the Texas Senate
Introduction of the Democratic Members of the Texas Senate
Dinner Music
  The Triolins
Introduction of Head Tables
Entrance of Lieutenant Governor Ben Barnes
Entrance of Governor and Mrs. Preston Smith
Welcome
  Elmer C. Baum, Chairman, State Democratic Executive Committee
Introduction of Lieutenant Governor Ben Barnes
  Mrs. Ralph S. O'Connor, Vice Chairman, State Democratic Executive Committee
Introduction of Governor Preston Smith
  H. H. Coffield, Secretary, State Democratic Executive Committee
Entertainment Master of Ceremonies
  Cactus Pryor
Entertainment
  Wayne Newton

DeeAnn always had a good time....

...visiting the House chamber.

My parents, Fannie and Tom Denton, attended my swearing in ceremony. My dad was born in 1898 in a log cabin in Falls County, Texas. His birthplace is now in a museum at Baylor University in Waco, Texas. They voted in every election.

Sissy Farenthold, John Bigham, Tom Moore, Lane Denton
This photo was taken after the historic vote that created the Dirty Thirty. Obviously, Sissy, who had spent countless hours making the case, was exhausted.

1.

On Monday, March 15, 1971, my life changed in a way that it would never be the same. That was the day I stood at the back microphone on the Floor of the House of Representatives in the Texas State Legislature and challenged one of the two most powerful men in Texas state politics, Speaker Gus Mutscher. It would be one of the most unique challenges of the powerful ruling forces in Texas ever made and something unheard of by a first-time legislator. The events that took place on that day began on January 12 of that year.

Two months before that life-changing event on the House Floor, I had been sworn in as a member of the 62nd Legislative Session of the Texas House of Representatives. I felt a certain chill as I walked up those same steps that Governor Sam Houston had ascended in 1861 when he opposed the succession of Texas from the United States and becoming a state within the Confederates States of the South. At fifteen years old, I had read John F. Kennedy's *Profiles in Courage*. He wrote of Sam Houston as "the most independent, unique, popular, forceful and dramatic individuals ever to serve in the United States Senate." As I was sworn into office on January 12, I was determined to walk in that man's footsteps and display the same quality as he did when he took on the forces of destruction more than one hundred ten years ago.

It was on that day in January, which was the same day that Governor Preston Smith was sworn in, that the Fort Worth Office of the Federal Securities and Exchange Commission (SEC) filed suit in federal court against Frank W. Sharp and an array of high-ranking businessmen and elected officials in the state legislature. Specifically, the Commission charged that Sharp had arranged private loans and stock purchases for House Speaker Gus Mutscher, Governor Preston Smith, House Appropriations Chairman W. S. "Bill" Heatly, State Representative Tommy Shannon, and two of Mutscher's aides. In return for the loans, Mutscher and his cronies agreed to expedite a special bill through the legislature to protect Sharp's interest in three banks and two insurance companies, all owned or controlled by him. The legislation was passed during a Special Session of the 61st Legislature in September 1969.

I sat in the special seating section for legislators viewing the swearing-in of the governor and lieutenant governor when word got to me that the charges had been filed just as Smith became our new governor. The House's session had begun on January 12 and Mutscher had been reelected as speaker for a second term. I had been sworn in as a first-term state representative from McLennan County, Texas.

The next day, I contacted Frances "Sissy" Farenthold, the only woman in the state legislature, and suggested that we must take advantage of this opportunity to challenge the power structure. She agreed, but we knew our numbers had to increase considerably for us to have any chance of winning this battle.

The plan was for us to request an official House investigation into the bribery charges included in the SEC suit against specifically those serving in the legislature. We also recognized that Speaker Mutscher would have never allowed us to utilize the normal legislative procedures to get that investigation. We had to develop an alternative plan.

[Document with signatures at top]

H.C.R. 87

WHEREAS, Information has been presented in the courts of the United States implying that certain persons have, directly or indirectly, given things of value, privilege, and personal advantage to Members of the Legislature of this state, intending thereby to influence them in the performance of their official duties; and

WHEREAS, Information has been presented in the courts of the United States implying that certain persons having a direct interest in a measure pending before, or thereafter to be introduced, in the Legislature of this state, did privately attempt to influence the actions of certain Members by methods other than by appealing to the reason of such Members; and

WHEREAS, Information has been presented in the courts of the United States implying that certain employed agents or representatives did privately endeavor to exercise influence over Members of the Legislature of this state concerning a measure then pending before such Legislature; and

WHEREAS, The preservation of popular confidence in the integrity of such a government is among the most solemn duties of a public official; and

WHEREAS, The indifference of inaction of this Legislature upon the presentation of information implying that corrupt practices have been exerted against certain of its Members could be viewed, and will understandably be viewed, as proof that the Government of Texas is not unswervingly committed to the best interests of those for whose benefit it has been instituted; and

WHEREAS, This Legislature has the right and duty to investigate any and all charges of undue influence against its Members; to pursue such charges until the truth be known; and to take such measures as may be necessary to prevent their repetition, all to the end that the Government of Texas may be rightly known as one whose officials act in no other interest than that of the people whom they serve; now therefore, be it

[Additional signatures at bottom]

H.C.R. 87 by Representative Sissy Farenthold allowed me to appeal the Speaker's ruling. Credit is given to Terrance O'Rourke and Glen Wilkerson for helping to draft the resolution.

We recruited more members to our cause. We knew our numbers were increasing, and we included the ultra-conservative Walter "Mad Dog" Mengden from Houston and liberal, flamboyant Curtis Graves from Houston. Our support covered the entire political spectrum from right to left, but we had one thing in common—to break the back of the conservative Democratic power brokers. We refused to accept the long tradition in the House—to "get along you had to go along." That simply meant that if you expected to get plum committee assignments or even assignments to those committees most important to your constituency, you had to go along with the leadership. In the case of the House, "don't rock the boat". This was especially true when it dealt with the charges in the SEC suit.

By February, we were meeting practically every night in Representative Tom Moore, Jr.'s office, gathering facts and planning a strategy. We recruited two very sharp volunteers, Glen Wilkerson and Terrence O'Rourke, who worked as Senate aides, to help in doing the research. O'Rourke and Wilkerson came across a tactic never used successfully in the House, but available to us. It was called "Privilege of the House," and allowed a member to call for the immediate consideration of a bill or resolution to investigate actions by members that denigrate the integrity of the House and its members.

Representative Sissy Farenthold agreed to offer the resolution but also knew Mutscher would gavel it "not privileged" and refuse to recognize her. We also figured he might not consider the possibilities of overriding his objection through another seldom-used tactic, and that would be to appeal the ruling of the Chair from the microphone at the back of the House Floor. According to House rules, in order to have my challenge recognized, I needed ten other members to second my motion. I immediately went to work in secret to recruit those ten members who would join our effort, fully aware that they would lose all possibility of getting their local as well as other bills important to their constituents passed. I visited regularly with ten members who I felt would stand up to the pressure from the speaker. After considerable cajoling and arm-twisting, we finally secured the ten who would second my motion.

When only ten of our secret team walked on the House Floor, none of the leadership had any idea what we planned to do. Most of the House members concentrated on their particular issues, giving very little attention to the pending suits against the leadership. Evidently, Mutscher's strategy was to say nothing about the suit and just wait it out with the belief it would go away. The establishment would not allow this to become an issue and would find ways to bury the suit.

There were two microphones on the House Floor: one below the speaker's podium, where he literally ruled over the proceedings, and one in the back of the chamber. As the session began, Sissy waited her turn at the front speaker. Finally, she walked up to the mike and spoke.

"I rise on a matter of privilege of the House to move the immediate consideration and adoption of House Concurrent Resolution 87, which calls for the establishment of a committee to investigate the charges brought by the Security and Exchange Commission against a member of the House of Representatives."

Pandemonium engulfed the House as loyalists to the speaker shouted insults at Sissy.

Others shouted, "Point of order! Point of order!"

A member in the back of the room closer to me raised his arm with a heavy book in his hands and prepared to throw it at Sissy, but held up when Mutscher banged the gavel down hard.

"Your motion is not privileged," he practically shouted at Sissy.

With his ruling, the chamber quieted.

Now it was my turn. As I stood to the right of the microphone, waiting to strike, I thought about Sam Houston back in December

1832 when he rode a mighty stallion into Texas and announced that he was about to enter Texas and his spirit was good and his heart was straight. I felt the same as I stepped to the mike and spoke.

"Mr. Speaker."

"Yes, Mr. Denton," Mutscher replied.

At that very moment, I crossed my fingers and hoped that Mutscher would not ask me why I sought recognition from the back microphone. If he had asked, he undoubtedly would have refused to recognize me when I answered. I waited momentarily and when that was not forthcoming, I knew we would win on this procedure.

"Mr. Speaker, I move to appeal the ruling of the Chair and I have the names of ten people who will second my motion."

Silence engulfed the House Floor. I knew the members were shocked that I had the audacity to challenge the ruling of the speaker. It was at that moment my future in Texas politics was sealed, signed, and delivered to me. Mutscher's glaring at me from behind the podium was enough to let me know he would not forget this intrusion into his power. However, at that moment, he had no choice but to follow procedure and respond to my request.

"I need for you to identify the ten members who are willing to second your motion," he dryly said.

I am sure the speaker never believed we would be able to get the ten seconds since taking that position would end a member's chances when pushing his legislative projects.

I hurried up to the podium and handed him the document containing the ten signatures of the members who had signed on as seconds. In order to expose them, he called out their names and asked each of them to stand.

"Tom Moore, Jr,. from Waco, Walter Mengen of Houston, David Allred from Wichita Falls (son of the thirty-third governor, James V. Allred), Dick Reed from Dallas, Nick Nichols of Houston, Curtis Graves of Houston, Reverend Zan Holmes from Dallas, John

Lane Denton & "The Dirty Thirty"

At the back microphone, waiting to see if the Speaker would recognize me. Only ten members were aware of what was about to happen. The courageous ten members who had signed, seconding the motion, which wiped out their legislative agenda in one vote—for open public government.

Bingham from Belton, Sissy Farenthold from Corpus, and Lane Denton from Waco."

We all stood and answered "Yes" when asked if we were signatories on the document. My appeal to the ruling was successful and history was made because it represented the first time a member had appealed the ruling of the chair.

Tom Moore, Jr., a member of our coalition, then rose to his feet and spoke.

"Point of order, Mr. Speaker. It is my understanding that the speaker must relinquish the chair while the appeal is debated."

As if stunned by Moore's words, Mutscher practically stumbled back from his position at the podium, turned, and looked at Bob Johnson, the Parliamentarian.

"Is that the rule of the House?" he asked.

Johnson did not say a thing, but simply nodded.

"Please get Representative Dewitt Hale up here," shouted an obviously irritated Mutscher.

I turned to Curtis, and we both smiled and realized we were in for a fight. We had temporarily won. Then I watched with great satisfaction as Hale made his way to the speaker's podium and Mutscher reluctantly handed him the gavel.

Confusion reigned momentarily as Mutscher's lieutenants made their way to the microphone in the front and attempted to protest what was happening to their leader, but Hale calmly brought the gavel down with a loud thud and forced the House back into order. I watched Mutscher make his way down from the speaker's podium, walk to the back of the chamber, and exit through the door.

The debate on my motion went on for three hours. For the first time in what some would claim the history of the chamber, every member was present on the Floor. Tom Moore and Curtis Graves gave dramatic speeches in support of my appeal. The excellent research provided by O'Rourke and Wilkerson provided us with all the facts needed for a winning argument. The Mutscher supporters had no facts to back up their positions. They simply argued that this procedure had never been effectively used in the House and it should not start now.

When Hale called for the vote, the pro-Mutscher forces prevailed, and we were defeated 118 to 30. Despite their victory, they were still in shock because they recognized this as the beginning of change in the Texas House of Representatives. Right after the vote, an extremely large lobbyist, wearing the typical lobbyist's white suit, leaned over the railing from the second tier and shouted.

Lane Denton & "The Dirty Thirty"

"The dirty bastards—those thirty dirty bastards."

Another visitor in the balcony shouted, "The dirty thirty."

Our label was born, and we would be recognized by that title for the rest of the session and into future sessions as well as Texas history. The thirty members who became the Dirty Thirty will go down in history and should receive a profile in courage award. They were: Fred Anguish, Dave Allred, Maurice Angly, Bill Bass, Tom Bass, John Bigham, Bill Blythe, Red Braun, Neil Caldwell, Tom Craddick, Lane Denton, Jim Earthman, Frances "Sissy" Farenthold, Bob Gammage, Ben Grant, Curtis Graves, John Hannah, Ed Harris, Fred Head, Zan Holmes, Edmond "Sonny" Jones, Walter Mengden, Tom Moore, Paul Moreno, Roy "Nick" Nichols, Charles Patterson, Dick Reed, Lindsey Rodriguez, Carlos Truan, and Bob Vale. Representative Dewitt Hale, acting as speaker, appointed Representative Dick Slack to notify Mutscher of the results and the speaker returned to the Floor to a standing ovation.

Returning to my office after that vote, I knew what probably lay ahead for me and the others now designated and therefore easily identifiable. What I did not know was just how vindictive Mutscher would be as we moved forward in the session.

Due to the press coverage and the public awareness of the scandal, Mutscher could not just gloat about his victory over our group. He had to make some attempt to resolve the issue to the satisfaction of the press. Days later, he addressed the entire House of Representatives in an attempt to exonerate himself by pointing out that he suffered losses in the stock transaction and therefore no corruption had taken place. To show some humility, he sounded quite disingenuous.

He said, "My family and I have been reassured and at the same time deeply moved by the faith and confidence you have so warmly demonstrated during this period of our lives. I say to you that your confidence has not been misplaced. I know the future will justify your faith."

In another disingenuous move, he established the House General Investigating Committee to further investigate the Sharpstown Scandal. The problem was all the members appointed to the Committee were strong Mutscher supporters. When he announced the creation of the Committee, I held out some hope that it would attempt to get to the bottom of the Sharpstown Scandal. I felt we had to assume that he would make it a panel that at least looked impartial. After all, if he took the trouble to go through the motions to create it, I thought he would put at least one Mutscher critic on the Committee just to make it look good. He appointed Representative Merton Murray as Chair, along with Representatives Hale, Nugent, Slider, and Haynes, all members who had signed pledge cards to support Mutscher in 1973 and 1975. The only action taken by the Committee during the session was to hold a meeting in which Chairman Murray instructed the other four members to cooperate with anyone gathering information in accordance with the Carl Parker Resolution.

Representative Carl Parker, who, at one time, had been a progressive labor leader, for some reason had switched allegiance and became a Mutscher loyalist. With strong support from the leadership, his resolution easily passed on the House Floor. It called for three state agencies, Attorney General's Office, the Banking Commission, and the Insurance Commission to join with two individuals, the President of the Texas Society of Certified Public Accountants and the Chairman of the Texas Society of Investment Bankers to investigate individually, the Sharpstown Scandal. The agencies and individuals were then to report any findings to the Attorney General, who then reported the findings to the House of Representatives. Needless to say, none of the individuals found anything.

Mutscher's final attempt to put on a face of concern over the Sharpstown Scandal was a bill introduced on the House Floor by

Jim Nugent, Chair of the Rules Committee. His bill was a real guise of an Ethics Bill. I found it rather incredulous that Nugent would even introduce such a bill. As Chairman of the Rules Committee, he had blocked all earlier reform efforts. I was correct in my assessment of the bill. It did nothing to rectify the most important problems confronting the corruption in the legislature and that was the enforcement of the laws already on the books. However, I thought if I could attach an amendment to his bill that put more teeth into the General Investigating Committee, the Dirty Thirty could support it.

Nugent's bill was scheduled to be voted on after the Easter recess. That gave me sufficient time to draft an amendment to his bill. I designed my amendment to address the weakness of the General Investigating Committee. The weakness was that all the members on the Committee were strong supporters of Mutscher. My amendment called for the members to be appointed by the entire House and not the speaker. One member would come from the minority party and committee membership would be allocated to representatives from both urban and rural districts.

I introduced my amendment the first day after the Easter recess. Nugent moved immediately to table it and he was successful. The House voted 103 to 47. The Ethics Bill, minus my amendment, passed with only seven votes against and one of those was mine. Now with the watered-down Ethics Bill and the Investigating Committee still intact with Mutscher supporters, the subject of the Sharpstown Scandal was put to rest for the rest of the session. Mutscher could now breathe much easier. He believed he was out of the woods and his chances for reelection and remain as speaker seemed firmly entrenched. That, however, was not the case and after the session ended, he would find out that his problems were far from over.

In March, the battle continued between Mutscher and those of us who had been targeted for defeat and removal from the legislature. It revolved around the issue between multi-member or single-member legislative districts. It began when a delegation of citizens from Garland, Texas, made a trip to the capitol to protest that they had no representation because of the multi-member district and how the members were chosen in Dallas County.

Garland, Texas, is a working, blue-collar city and not a part of the downtown Dallas business leaders who saw no reason for them to have a representative. They met with me in my office and urged my support for single-member districts and one district that would accommodate their political interests. They explained that Dallas County was under the control of the Dallas Citizens Council and the powerful business lobby. They chose the slate to fill the legislative seats for the district. And they always won. The situation was so bad, one of the chosen few elected in 1970 admitted that he was in France during the time to run for re-election, never campaigned, and was still re-elected. The group from Garland made a big pitch for a change to single-member districts and heavily lobbied the Capitol.

Mutscher adamantly opposed the change to single-member districts and had his man, Delwin Jones, chair the Redistricting Committee. He made it quite clear to the Garland constituency, the Dirty Thirty, and some Republicans that the new boundaries would be designed as multi-member. To convert to single-member districts, he argued, would bring the Chicago-type ward politics to Texas.

With little advance notice, Jones held only two committee meetings and no advance notice was given regarding the time and place. It became clear that the Conservative Democrats from Dallas, Harris County, and Bexar County were running the show. The Republicans were totally ignored. Sonny Jones and Bill Blythe, two Republican members, submitted legislation for single-member districts and it was ignored, buried in committee. Bob Davis tried to introduce legislation that would specifically break Harris County into single members, and it, too, was rejected. Reverend Zan Holmes

Lane Denton & "The Dirty Thirty"

The Dirty Thirty took on the unconstitutional redistributing bill. Harvey Katz arrived on the scene at my request. My friend, Robert B. Choate, helped fund his expenses.

from Dallas told the powers in that city that if they did not agree for Dallas County to have single-member districts, he would withhold the Black vote from the approved slate in 1972. His threats fell on deaf ears. Tom Bass and Dick Reed offered a Constitutional Amendment to go to the voters to amend the Constitution and require 150 separate legislative districts. Their amendment never came up for a vote. Mutscher was in absolute control and had the votes to get his way.

It was late in May, and no one had yet seen the proposed redistricting legislation. But rumors spread that Tom Moore and I were at the top of the list to be eliminated, or at least one of us would lose. With four days left in the session, the bill came up for consideration on May 26. When Jones sauntered onto the House Floor with the revised map with the recommended changes, he was swamped by members. Everyone wanted to find out how they would be affected by the redistricting. Representative Jones only released one copy of the bill.

Just as I had expected, the committee had maintained the multi-districts but manipulated the districts in such a way that the Dirty Thirty were paired against each other wherever possible. They drew the lines so that Tom Moore and I were pitted against each other. When Tom looked at the map, he said, "This reeks of piss and I'm mad as hell." The same was true for other members of our group. Mutscher's goal was to eliminate as many progressives and independent Democrats as possible and that led to our quite different ideologies joining forces against the ruling group. Even Representative Bill Finch from San Antonio, a friend and famous for giving free Finch cigars to everyone in the Capitol, and had supported Mutscher all the way, said, "We're going to burn this S.O.B."

Despite the overwhelming odds against us, we continued the fight. Dick Reed and Tom Bass tried to get a pledge from Mutscher. If he would do single-member districts, they would help get the vote for his top priority legislation, liquor by the drink, passed. Mutscher was not about to buy off on that deal since he knew he had the votes to pass his legislation without their help. And he was committed to keeping the multi-member districts if for no other reason than to eliminate some of his opposition.

Bill Heatly, Chair of Appropriations Committee, slipped in an amendment that added two hundred thousand dollars to be dispersed to the Attorney General. Mutscher knew the redistricting was going to be challenged in the courts by many different interest groups, so he made sure the Attorney General had the additional resources to argue for the state.

Our only hope to stave off this tragedy was to begin a delaying tactic. Under the Texas Constitution, the Legislature can only meet for 150 days. To extend, a session must be done by the governor. We introduced dozens of amendments and encouraged those outside our circle to do the same. Fred Head, a Dirty Thirty member, made a motion to delay, and it was tabled. Rex Braun and Dave Allred raised a point of order and forced a recess for two and a half hours. Neal Caldwell, along with Tom Bass, also attempted to raise a point of order and were denied.

As we neared the midnight hour, confusion reigned on the House Floor. The situation grew increasingly tense and finally, Department of Public Safety Officers (DPS) marched into the House chamber and stood at the entrance and the exit doors.

The nineteen members from Harris County continued to wage a fight for single-member districts. Curtis Graves got up and gave a strong speech. He said, "If you leave Harris County as multi-districts, you are eventually going to have four Black Panthers with Afros two feet high in here, raising hell all the time." I helped elect two members in 1972 with Afros, Mickey Leland and Craig Washington, two of the best legislators in Texas legislative history.

Tom Bass grabbed the microphone and shouted, "Mr. Speaker, I'll play by the rules if you recognize me and if you don't, you're going to have to have the Sergeant of Arms remove me because I'm going to create a disturbance."

Just as Bass finished shouting, several heated arguments exploded on the Floor. Things got quite ugly. Mutscher repeatedly banged his gavel down, but to no avail. Finally, he agreed to allow Rex Braun to give a personal privilege speech. Bass followed him and gave one, as did DeWitt Hale. And then the most dramatic action happened when Graves offered an amendment and then turned to the speaker and said, "In my amendment, I include Huntsville, the main facility for the prisons system, in your district because that's where you're going real soon." His amendment lost in a 103 to 30 vote.

As time neared midnight, I noticed the gallery remained packed and most of the people supported single-member districts and appreciated what the Dirty Thirty attempted to accomplish. Finally, just a few minutes before midnight, Representative Hilary Doran from Del Rio moved the previous question and called for the final vote. Just as we voted, DPS announced that there was a bomb threat, and the Capitol was being evacuated, so we cast our vote and got out of the building. We would not know the outcome until the next day, which was Saturday. When we arrived at the Capitol, the word had spread that the Mutscher-Jones Redistricting Bill had passed the House of Representatives by a vote of 93 to 52. Temporarily, I was pitted against Tom Moore. However, he decided to run for the state Senate seat and that left me with token opposition for the 1972 election.

As we all prepared to leave the chambers, Republican Bill Blythe from Houston got up and said, "We fought the Alamo last night and we lost. But remember, Harris County is the site of the Battle of San Jacinto where Texans won their freedom again and Harris County will win its freedom again."

Blythe's prediction would ultimately materialize, but not through the very conservative controlled Texas Legislature. A few days after the final passage of the Mutscher-Jones Bill, the United States Supreme Court ordered Hinds County, Mississippi, to convert to single-member districts. Two weeks later, the Texas Supreme Court ruled the Mutscher-Jones Bill unconstitutional and permanently enjoined the Secretary of State from holding elections under that statute. Redistricting was sent to the Redistricting Legislative Board.

On May 30, I rose to make a personal privilege speech.

After I concluded my remarks, Representative Vernon Beckham from Denison, and one of the most conservative members, came over and told me that he admired my courage and would like to have his picture taken with me. With that gesture, I knew the legislature was beginning to change.

Finally, on May 31, the 62nd Legislative Session came to an end. During those 150 days of acrimony and turbulence, a beleaguered Mutscher essentially found a way to win the myriad of battles with

Addressing the House on matters of personal privilege.

the Dirty Thirty, but we refused to go out with only a whimper. Twenty-one of us refused to sign the customary resolution honoring the speaker for a job well done. We also refused to attend the Speaker's Day Celebration. Instead, we held our own end-of-session party, hosted by Sissy Farenthold at Schultz's Beer Garden. We were putting the speaker and all his cohorts on notice that they may have won the initial battle, but the war was not yet over.

After my personal privilege speech, Representative Vernon Beckman, one of the most conservative members, thanked me and asked if I would have my photo with him. I considered him a friend.

resent the people of my county, and have deprived many of you of your right to represent the people of Texas.

Members, the blame is so heavy and diffuse for this destruction of the public interest that it is difficult for me to make a specific accusation. There are men in this room who have been accused of disregarding any notion of public duty, of using their office and the Membership of this House to further their own personal ambition and private financial interests. These men have defended themselves so ineptly against these charges that the public is not only questioning their integrity but their intelligence as well. And Members, with each public question, with each public doubt about one of these men, your reputation and mine suffers as well. But I cannot blame these men without blaming many of those who have defended their abuses.

Perhaps there is enough politician in me to forgive those who have compromised in order to help constructive legislation. But those of you whose price has been another park or such for your districts know in your hearts that you have not deserted reform out of any sense of public duty, but that your sole objective has been to maintain this legislature as a private club in which you are assured a lifetime membership. Ultimately, I must place the greatest blame on those of you who came here with stars in your eyes, who joined the fight for honest representation in the past and who have suddenly become the loudest defenders of those who abuse their office. You are the ones who know better. You cover your hypocrisy with jokes and evasions, but you don't fool very many of us.

Believe me, gentlemen, I will not leave here feeling like a saint. I cannot count the times that young people came to me and pleaded with me to fight again and I was too tired and too discouraged to rise one more time. I will leave this session feeling that there may have been more I should have done. I intend to run on my record.

On the other hand, I feel much better about myself and those who stood with me Friday night. You have the votes, but we have respect for the people of this state. We trust those at the press table to tell the people what has happened here and we trust the people to understand and to rebel against this tyranny of self-interest. And I tell you now, that we will take that respect and that trust to the people of Texas, to every corner of this state. And I do believe that the people are going to tear the map you drew last night to shreds and elect a legislature of which Texas can be proud.

May 30, personal privilege speech.

Lane Denton

1088　　　　　　HOUSE JOURNAL

HCR 87—MOTION TO CONSIDER

Mrs. Farenthold moved, as a matter of privilege, to take up and consider at this time, HCR 87.

The Speaker did not recognize Mrs. Farenthold on the motion stating that the resolution was not privileged under Rule 17 of the House Rules and the resolution cannot be considered at this time.

Mr. Denton appealed from the ruling of the Chair.

The appeal was seconded by Representatives Denton, Tom Moore, Jr., Mengden, Farenthold, Allred, Reed, Nichols, Graves, Zan Holmes, and Bigham.

Mr. Hale was called to the Chair pending the appeal.

(Mr. Hale in the Chair)

March 15, 1971　　　HOUSE JOURNAL　　　1089

Nays—30

Agnich	Caldwell	Hannah, John	Nichols
Allred	Craddick	Harris	Patterson
Angly	Denton	Head	Reed
Bass, B.	Earthman	Holmes, Z.	Rodriguez
Bass, T.	Farenthold	Jones, E.	Truan
Bigham	Gammage	Mengden	Vale
Blythe	Grant	Moore, T.	
Braun	Graves	Moreno	

In The Chair

Hale

The Capital Press wanted to see the list of members voting "no."

The Dirty Thirty group planning amendments to the Appropriation bill. This was the first time in history that a group of members offered over one hundred amendments.

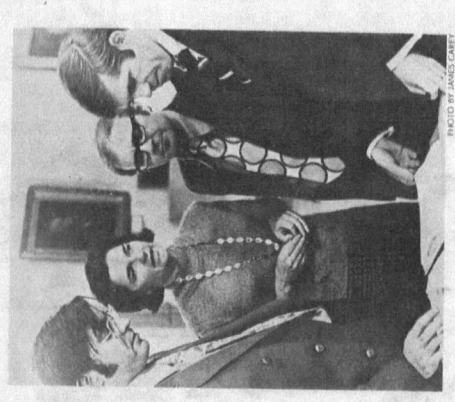

Katz's book was on the bestseller's list, under contract for paperback and a movie. A Texas oil tycoon funded a libel lawsuit, which stopped everything. Three years later, Texas Supreme Court ruled in favor of Katz and Doubleday.

Lane Denton & "The Dirty Thirty"

Representative Fred Head wanted a group photo of the Dirty Thirty members, the last day of the 62nd Legislature. Could not get all 30 together. A task that even Representative Head could not could not accomplish.

A group of Baylor Young Democrats presenting plans for banquet honoring the "Dirty 30."

A sell out event—over 1,000 people present to honor the "Dirty 30."

After the Baylor Young Democrats event, Sissy and I visited with Barry Bryant, Molly Ivins, and Harvey Katz. Harvey was violating the rules at Baylor's Student Union and Baylor. You cannot smoke on campus.

Lane Denton & "The Dirty Thirty"

Over fifty years ago, I took on a controversial issue that is still important today.

Prohibiting cash bail for misdemeanor charges. Citizens should not be penalized because they are poor.

I introduced HJR 13 in 1971 with Representatives Curtis Graves, Dick Reed, Carlos Truman, and Tom Moore, Jr., making it illegal to require bail for misdemeanor cases.

Powerful forces keep citizens locked up. America has a very unfair bail/bond system. A system that works for bail/bond companies and prison/jail systems, but not for the ordinary Americans. Money is the controlling force.

A case that made national news was Sandra Bland, a twenty-eight-year-old African-American woman found hanged in a jail cell in Waller County, Texas, on July 13, 2015, three days after being arrested because she refused to put out her cigarette. Her family was trying to post $500 to bail her out.

If you are wealthy, you walk out immediately from jail. People should not be kept in jail because they are poor.

2.

Immediately after the legislative session adjourned, I looked forward to the election in 1972 and to how best our group could take advantage of all the turmoil and confusion created around the Sharpstown Scandal. I knew the key to next year's election would be an emphasis on reform. The people were fed up with what was happening in Austin, and we received a big boost from the *Houston Post*. Two of the writers did a great job keeping the events in the Capital City before the people. Felton West was the chief reporter for the paper in Austin, and Henry Holcombe was his assistant. They did a weekly play-by-play coverage of the continuous Sharpstown Scandal and the calls for reform.

In June, I sought advice from Tom Moore, the one man who probably knew the political terrain in Texas as well as anyone, about our chances of winning control of the House under the banner of the Dirty Thirty. According to Tom, the time would have never been better to throw the rascals out than in the 1972 elections.

Two decisions made by federal courts convinced me that there would be a major revision in the electoral process in Texas. The first decision came from the federal district court in Mississippi when it ruled multi-member districts in that state were unconstitutional. The second occurred when the federal court in Austin tossed out the Mutscher Redistricting Legislation and sent it to the Legislative

Redistricting Board for revisions. Even though I knew the Board would probably not draft a new plan that changed the structure from multi-member to single-member districts, I figured, ultimately, the court would also reject their plan. The trend seemed to have been bending in favor of single-member districts, and we needed to lay out our electoral plans with that in mind.

By September, events happened that would also influence the 1972 elections. All these events were encouraging to the Dirty Thirty. On September 2, the *Associated Press* reported that Travis County Grand Jury would indict Mutscher, Shannon, and the Speaker's aide, Rush McGinty, on criminal charges. On September 23, the indictments were officially filed. Mutscher became the highest state official to be charged with a felony since Governor James "Pa" Ferguson was impeached in 1917. Mutscher and the others were charged with accepting a bribe and conspiracy to accept a bribe.

Soon after the announcement of the indictment, Mutscher made it noticeably clear that he did not plan to step down as Speaker. He reasoned that since the Legislative Redistricting Board was now responsible for drawing up new districts and he was a member of that Board as Speaker, he could not legally delegate his position.

I challenged his reasoning, as did other members of the Dirty Thirty. Early in October, we held a press conference in Austin, along with David Allred and Tom Moore, Jr., who had requested the Governor call the House into session so we could vote to remove Mutscher. Governor Smith refused to accommodate our request. Mutscher remained Speaker and participated with the other four members of the Board, including the Lieutenant Governor, Attorney General, Comptroller, and Commissioner of the General Land Office. All these men, except Bob Armstrong, shared a common political outlook, and we knew whatever plan they developed would not call for single-member districts. We only hoped the Courts would also reject their plan.

Walter H. Mengden, Tom Moore, Jr., Dave Allred, and I outlining the plan for the Dirty Thirty election campaign. I was selected as the chair for our election campaign.

The Dirty Thirty sent a questionnaire to every candidate for the Texas House of Representatives. It helps to have candidates on the record. This helped our group elect seventy-six new members and, in 1973, pass historic public government laws.

Early in December, the Mutscher trial was moved out of Austin to Abilene, Texas. Their lawyers had successfully argued that there was no way they could get a fair trial in the politically charged environment of the state Capitol. The lawyer assumed that the folks far removed from Austin would not be biased against their clients, as they assumed would be the case in Austin.

With the trial date set for February and all activity moved to Abilene, and with the new redistricting plan before the Court waiting for a decision, we all took a break from the turbulence and enjoyed the holiday season. I finally found some time to spend with my wife, Betty, and daughter, DeeAnn, as well as visit my brothers and sisters. It was a welcomed break and rest from the nonstop confrontations of the past year. I knew right after New Year, I would be back in rare form, anticipating the election of a new 150-member House of Representatives, and a new governor and lieutenant governor for the next legislative session in 1973.

It did not take long for the action on the home front to heat up. On January 28, a three-judge federal court in Austin struck down the Legislative Redistricting Board's plan for apportioning the districts in the House. The judges found that the use of multi-member districts in every metropolitan area, except Houston, was not equal. Witnesses before the judges testified that multi-member districts were much too expensive for most candidates because they had to run in very widespread geographical areas with an overwhelming number of white voters and that diluted the voting strength of Blacks, Mexican Americans, and even Republicans. As a result, slates of candidates in these districts, put up by financially powerful coalitions, dominated the electoral process.

This ruling was exactly what we had been waiting for since the infamous Mutscher Redistricting Bill passed in the legislature. We knew our chances of success in the upcoming election just grew by leaps and bounds. It was time for the Dirty Thirty to go to work.

My first goal was to get the original Dirty Thirty back together. Although some of our group were running for other offices than what they held in the state legislature, they all agreed to help. Sissy planned on running for governor as the reform candidate. I pledged my full support to her candidacy. Even though I would dedicate most of my time and energy to changing the face of the House, I knew I could carve out some time to assist her. We knew her chances of winning were difficult. We were still excited about Texas electing its first female governor since Miriam "Ma" Ferguson back in 1922. Sissy defeated the incumbent governor and lieutenant governor, placing her in a runoff with billionaire Dolph Briscoe, who ultimately won.

One of the key members of our group, Tom Moore, ran for State Senate, and Curtis Graves was challenging Barbara Jordan for a new congressional seat in the Houston area. Tom Bass sought a County Commissioner's seat in Houston and Dick Reed did the same in Dallas. Still, they all pledged their support to assist in our attempt to change the face of the House of Representatives in Austin.

Our goal was to recruit candidates who agreed with our agenda for reform. However, this created some problems for our team. Many of the candidates that we might support might challenge our colleagues in the House, seeking reelection to their seats. If the old guard had won, that could have created a great deal of bad blood during the 1973 legislative session, but that did not deter our efforts to move forward. Many of the so-called colleagues were still strong Mutscher supporters and not supporters of reform. We owed them no allegiance.

The other concern expressed by the reform group was that we would go up against the most entrenched money lobbyists and corporate groups, not only in Texas but across the country. With all the oil and gas and insurance interests, as well as the State and National Chamber of Commerce fighting us with all the resources they could muster, we had our work cut out for us. The battle would have been worth it if the result was victory and a new look in Austin.

In early February, I called a meeting in Austin of the original group of thirty. Even those who had committed to running for other offices in the state showed up. I was nominated and chosen chairman and the Dirty Thirty now took on a formal structure. I asked Dick Reed, Charles Patterson, Tom Moore, John Bigham, and Sissy Farenthold to serve as my steering committee, and they agreed. Tom Bass allowed us to utilize his assistant, Karen Learner. Madelyn Olds also served as our coordinator and assisted with organizing for the 1972 elections.

While we were organizing to take on the Mutscher forces, we received a gift from what was happening up in Abilene. On February 29, the trial began. I was confident the jurors would do the right thing and deliver a guilty verdict. These men had mortgaged their offices for financial gain and lost the public's trust. They had to pay for that betrayal. Even though the trial had been moved out of Austin, and the Sharpstown Scandal had received so much publicity, there was no way the four men and eight women jurors in Abilene did not know the magnitude of their responsibility to all the citizens of Texas.

The prosecution built their case on four key points: 1) They communicated the need and desire of Sharp for favorable legislation, 2) The solicitation of money by Mutscher for the favorable legislation, 3) The passage of Sharp's favorable bill through the House, and 3) Immediate profit made by the defendants on their stock in National Bankers Life.

On March 14, after calling over a dozen witnesses to include Frank Sharp, who had turned state's evidence and taking on some of the best attorneys that money could hire, the prosecution rested their case. To everyone's surprise, the defense did not call on any witnesses. Instead, they rested their case. They argued that the prosecution had failed to prove their case and that the jury should immediately return not guilty verdicts.

The defense attorneys got what they asked for and that was a quick deliberation, but not with the outcome they expected. After two and a half hours of deliberation, the jury returned a guilty verdict against all three defendants. The very next day, March 15, which marked a year since Sissy's resolution was introduced and my challenge to the speaker occurred, the judge sentenced all three to five-year prison sentences but probated so they would not serve prison time. The guilty verdict of the speaker, the second most powerful politician in the state, had profound implications for the upcoming election, and for that reason, I was quite satisfied with the outcome. All over the state, angry voters were just waiting for May 6 so they could also cast their ballots against corruption in Austin. I was ready to accommodate them by providing candidates they could support who were not part of that corruption.

Our first goal was to draft a questionnaire as a basis for determining what candidates we would support. Initially, there was some conflict as to who should receive our questions. Some members felt we should publicly endorse candidates in all of the races, even if they did not respond to our questionnaire. I felt we should only support candidates who sought our endorsement by responding to the questions. My position prevailed. We then sent the questionnaires to only those candidates who reached out to us for support. However, as our credibility continued to grow, other candidates contacted us.

As an organization, we were cash poor and did not expect to get any money from the sources that support various organizations and candidates going into an election year. We didn't have an office or a telephone. We only had a burning desire to win this battle against the forces that controlled the state. We produced a bumper sticker that read, "Reform the Legislature," and it became popular across the state. Early on, we recognized the strategy was to continue to pound the issue of reform and that our position against Mutscher's corruption, which was symbolic of the deep-seated corruption within the state, had been vindicated by the results in the trial in Abilene.

With a guilty verdict and Mutscher now a convicted felon, there was no doubt that he would have to resign as speaker. On March 21, he turned in his resignation but did not give up his seat in House. He also announced that he would not preside over the session to replace him. Since he continued serving in the House as a member, we knew then that he probably planned to run for reelection.

Mutscher's final act as speaker was to appoint Representative James Slider from Naples as the acting speaker to oversee the election. All 150 members were on the House floor as Slider read Mutscher's resignation letter. The House then addressed a procedural issue: whether the vote for a new speaker should be by secret ballot.

Representative Parker immediately introduced HSR #1, which called for an election by secret ballot. Representatives Don Cavness and Frank Calhoun offered an amendment to Parker's resolution, calling for a public roll call vote with all votes to be recorded and entered into the *House Journal*. Sissy then offered an amendment to the Cavness and Calhoun amendment that would have established a ten-member nominating committee to be chosen by the House, acting as a Committee of the Whole. The committee would then submit to the membership, at least three names, and then additional names would be permitted from the floor. Wasting no time, Parker then moved to table Sissy's amendment, and he was successful with a 111-36 vote. He then also moved to table the Cavness-Calhoun Amendment, but was not successful this time. The vote was 119-28 not to table. The final procedural outcome was that the election of the new temporary speaker would be by public ballot and recorded with nominations from the floor. We then got on to the nominations.

Ed Howard from Texarkana was the first to his feet and nominated Rayford Price. In his nomination comments, he considered Price was the only candidate who stood for reform and, according to Howard, Price was the only man who could restore public confidence in the system that had been severely damaged by the Sharpstown scandal. Once Howard sat back down, Tom Bass, in a surprising move to all of us, jumped up and nominated L. DeWitt Hale. He then attempted to justify his nomination. He told us he would like nothing more than to nominate a member of the Dirty Thirty. However, realistically, he felt the Dirty Thirty would have served its purpose if the House adopted meaningful reform rules, something more important than who was the speaker. He finally told us it was with some reservations that he nominated Hale.

In an unanticipated move, Tom Moore, almost in defiance of Bass, nominated Zan Holmes, a member of the Dirty Thirty. In nominating Holmes, Moore argued that the choice between Price and Hale was no choice at all for those seeking reform. Price was the overwhelming choice of the Texas Manufacturers Association and the oil and chemical industries, and Hale was busy trying to put the old Mutscher machine back together. Neither one of the two candidates represented the kind of reform the legislature was seeking to support. I also got up and supported Zan, telling the members that "Holmes was a man with a proven record for reform—a man of Christian values and ethics. We do not need warmed-over politicians of a yesterday."

On the first ballot, Price received 67 votes, Hale 50, Holmes 17, Hawkins Menefee 10, and James Nugent 1. The Dirty Thirty divided their votes with 6 for Price, 10 for Hale, 11 for Holmes, and 3 for Menefee. Since no one candidate received a majority vote, we held a runoff between Price and Hale. In that vote, Price received 77 and 65 for Hale. We split our votes, giving 8 to Price, 20 to Hale, and two members of the Dirty Thirty abstained. Until the 1973 legislative session, Price was the speaker but would again have to face another election if he were sent back to the legislature for the new session.

Mutscher's fall from grace continued on June 3 in the primary election. He lost his reelection bid to Latham Boone III, 11,119 to 8,614. His career was now over, and it all began back in February 1972, when Sissy Farenthold challenged him on the legislative floor about his involvement in the Sharpstown Scandal. It took a long time, but finally, justice had prevailed.

Finally, in fall 1972, the victory we sought back in the summer of 1971 finally became a reality. Two major events led to an overwhelming onslaught by the "Reform" movement candidates. The first event was on January 28, when the three-judge federal court struck down the multi-member districts and insisted the new legislative districts be drawn up as single-member. A great deal of credit for that change goes to State Senators Oscar Mauzy and A.R. (Babe) Schwartz, long-time supporters of single-member districts who kept the issue alive and well until the court finally ruled in favor of the single-member districts. Enormous credit also must be given to Federal Judge William Wayne Justice of East Texas, a member of the three-judge panel. He took the lead, arguing in favor of single-member districts.

The other major event that led to our overwhelming victory was the great amount of attention given to the Sharpstown Scandal and the corruption associated with it. The voters of Texas were ready for some serious reform, and we offered them the candidates that represented change. The reform movement, coupled with the court decision, brought seventy-six new members to the Texas House of Representatives. Besides Mutscher, the other defeated incumbents included Speaker Rayford Price losing to a Dirty Thirty member, Fred Head, in a scathing battle, which meant we would have a new speaker for the 1973 session. Immediately, the leading candidate was Price Daniel, Jr. As we prepared to move on to the new session, we knew reform would dominate the session, and we knew Daniel was committed to a reform agenda. Finally, the citizens of Texas would get what they so desperately needed, and that was a corrupt-free government.

Lane Denton

The "Dirty Thirty" Legislative Questionnaire

I. **Legislative Conference Committees**
During the last session of the Legislature the Conference Committee on Appropriations added over $21,000,000, unauthorized by either the House or the Senate, to the General Appropriations Bill. This Conference Committee met at times and places unknown to the membership of the House and when the Conference Committee report was brought to a vote, debate was shut off by the leadership.

YES NO
/X/ /_/ 1. I will support provisions to limit the powers of Conference Committees to adjustment of differences between House and Senate versions of a bill.
/X/ /_/ 2. I will support open meetings of all major Conference Committees (i.e. Appropriations, Taxes, Redistricting, etc.), and adequate advance notice of such meetings.
/X/ /_/ 3. I will support extended debate on all major Conference Committee reports.

II. **Legislative Committees**
For many years the Speaker of the House has used the existing committee structure as a vehicle to maintain almost dictatorial control of the House. Each session every committee has had almost entirely new membership thus preventing the members from getting any experience in the legislative area in which they are dealing. Some chairmen have used assignment of the bills to sub-committee (all bills going automatically to sub-committees) composed of three or four members that they control as a further means of killing legislation.

/X/ /_/ 1. I support a system of limited seniority on House Committees. (This system would allow for sustained membership on committees with the Speaker appointing a new chairman each session.)
/X/ /_/ 2. I support a reduction in the number of House Committees with each member serving on only two committees. (This would eliminate unnecessary committees, bring less important committees under the jurisdiction of major ones.)
/_/ /X/ 3. I support permanent year around staffing of all committees.
/X/ /_/ 4. I support a system of allowing five days written notice of all bills to be heard before a committee.
/X/ /_/ 5. I support the keeping of a public record of all votes taken in committee.

III. **Unethical Conduct**
/X/ /_/ 1. I support financial disclosures, under oath, by each legislator of sources and amounts of income to self and immediate family and value of all property owned by self, immediate family and corporations in which he or members of his immediate family hold at least 10% interest.
/X/ /_/ 2. I support disclosures by each lobbyist of all clients, amounts of fees for each client, amounts spent by self for each cleint on lobbying, and how each amount was spent.
/X/ /_/ 3. I support disclosure by each candidate of all amounts contributed to campaign whether before or after candidacy announcement or filing date, how all amounts were spent, identity of all contributors, including membership in organizations of contributing groups.
/X/ /_/ 4. I support the creation of an enforcement agency or special division of the Attorney General's Office with adequate staff and appropriation to investigate all disclosure statements, all possible misconduct by state officials, and to refer all violations to the district attorney for prosecution.
/_/ /X/ 5. I support clarification of criminal statutes to provide that false statements, under oath to state officials constitute a felony.
/_/ /X/ 6. I support clarification of criminal statutes to provide that failure to file disclosure statements by lobbyists, officials, or candidates constitutes a felony.

** THIS QUESTIONAIRE MUST BE RETURNED BY MARCH 24, 1972

Lane Denton & "The Dirty Thirty"

Dirty Thirty Questionnaire
page 2

IV. The Speakership

✓ / ☐ 1. I support complete abandonment of the pledge system for Speaker candidates.
☐ / ✓ 2. I support the limitation of the Speakership to one consecutive term
✓ / ☐ 3. I support a requirement for the Speaker's office to maintain a public record of all visitors to the office and all telephone calls made or received, to be verified by the Speaker, under oath, and filed with the Secretary of State.
✓ / ☐ 4. I support disclosure by each candidate for Speaker of the House of Representatives of all amounts contributed to campaign whether before or after candidacy announcement or filing date, how all amounts were spent, identity of all contributors, including membership in organizations of contributing groups.

V. The Legislators

For many years the House Contingency Expense Fund has been used as a vehicle by the Speaker for control or censorship of House members. This fund provides for the staffing and other expenses incurred by the Legislature both during sessions and during interim periods.

✓ / ☐ 1. I support providing one full time staff aid, one full time secretary and one part-time staff aid to each member of the House.
✓ / ☐ 2. I support removal of all discriminatory limitations on the use of printing and mailing allotments by House members.
✓ / ☐ 3. I support a three minute advance notice of all roll call votes. (This is to prohibit the quick call and allow all members reasonable time to return to their desks and to be sure of issues voted upon.)

I would like to clarify some of my answers as follows:
IV.-2. With the other proposed restrictions upon the Speaker, I do not see the necessity to limit him to one term. I feel this is an unnecessary reaction to a particularly bad problem. However, please understand that I am strongly and firmly committed to workable substantial reform not only in the Legislature but throughout the entire range of government in Texas.

Are you presently committed or pledged to any candidate for Speaker of the Texas House of Representatives, 63rd Session? If so, to whom:
NO

Is there any announced candidate (or candidates) for Speaker of the Texas House of Representatives, 63rd Session, that you could support or vote for as the next Speaker? If so, who:
Possibly Price Daniel, Jr. or Fred Head

I would like you to consider me:
✓ a. For public endorsement by The "Dirty Thirty", or
✓ b. For "Dirty Thirty" assistance and support during the campaign, or
✓ c. Possible membership in a reform caucus in the 63rd Legislature.

Signature: ▓▓▓▓▓▓▓▓

Please print:

Name: ▓▓▓▓▓▓▓▓

District: ▓▓▓▓▓▓▓▓

Date: 3-21-72

**Please return to:

The "Dirty Thirty"
P. O. Box 13086
Austin, Texas 78711

** THIS QUESTIONAIRE MUST BE RETURNED BY MARCH 24, 1972

(Not Printed at State Expense)

Lane Denton

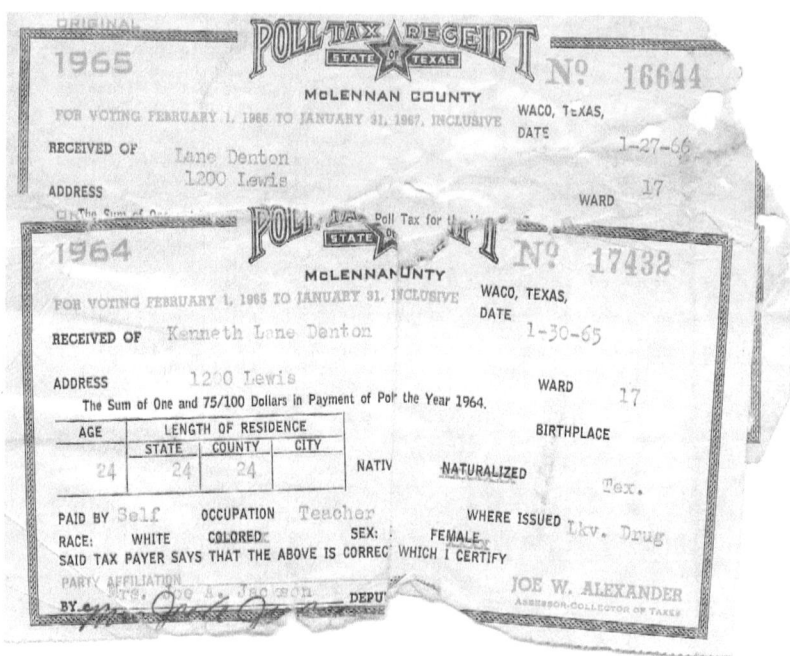

Voting has never been easy.

Lane Denton & "The Dirty Thirty"

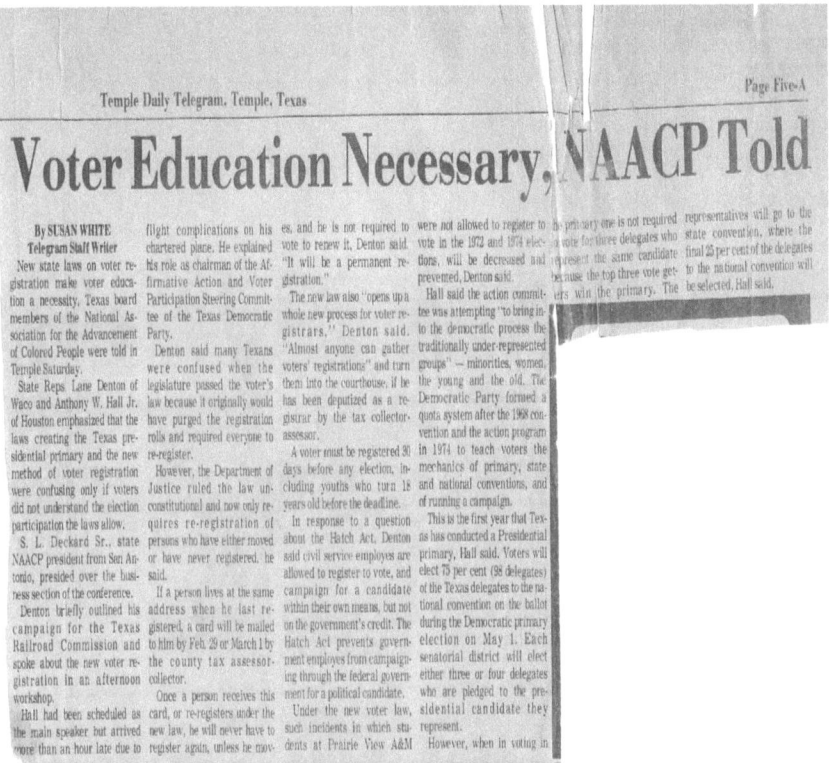

In 1972 and 1974, students at Prairie View A&M (predominately Black university) were not allowed to vote.

Along with other members of the Texas House, we fought the county and won the right to register for the students.

In 2020, ninety-two million Americans did not vote. We must urge every American to participate and vote.

Lane Denton

What made President Lyndon B. Johnson special was the ability to put his arms around your shoulders and look directly into your eyes. An invitation to the ranch (an LBJ BBQ) was always a special event.

Lyndon Johnson started teaching at age twenty in Cotulla, Texas. President Johnson passed historic health care, voting, and significant educational laws. The most comprehensive of any president in history.

It's difficult to understand that President Johnson, in less than a year, would die of a heart attack.

Lane Denton & "The Dirty Thirty"

Betty and I with a group of Texas House members enjoying a plate of barbecue on the Pedernales River (a very hot summer day).

Explaining the details of H.B.6, open records law, which I authored as part of reform legislation. This legislation is recognized as the most significant legislation in Texas Legislative history.

Governor Dolph Briscoe came on the House floor to congratulate me on the passage of H.B.6. The governor thanked me for getting the legislation passed.

3.

We began the 63rd Legislative Session in 1973, confident that considerable changes would be implemented throughout state government. Our hard work during the 1972 election had paid off. It was now our legislature. The reform movement had brought in seventy-six new members to the Texas House of Representatives, the biggest turnover in the history of the House. In Harris County alone, we elected eighteen new members. Out of that eighteen, we also elected four Blacks: Mickey Leland, Craig Washington, Anthony Hall, and Senfronia Thompson. The four and a young Vietnam veteran, Ben Reyes, turned out to be some of the best of that rookie group.

Because of the large number of new members supported by the Dirty Thirty, we controlled who would be the next speaker of the House since Rayford Price had been surprisingly beaten by Fred Head, one of the leaders of the Dirty Thirty. Our choice for the speakership was Price Daniel, Jr., the thirty-one-year-old son of former House Speaker, United States Senator, Attorney General, and governor, Price Daniel, Sr. He had first been elected back in 1968 and was considered a moderate liberal. Even though he did not support the Farenthold Resolution in the 62nd, he supported most of the issues of the Dirty Thirty during that session. He also promised to serve only one term as the speaker and was committed to supporting a strong ethics bill applicable to all state officials. In fact, he was on board for an entire package of reforms.

I had known Price at Baylor University, where he earned a law degree, so we were on familiar terms when the session was called to order on January 9, 1973. I met with the assumed-to-be new speaker before the session began. He promised to appoint those members loyal to the Dirty Thirty as chairs of committees to navigate the important reform legislation to be considered during the session. He also asked me what committee I wanted to chair. I told him I preferred not to chair a specific committee because if you are a committee chair, you must devote most of your time and resources there.

I wanted to coordinate, with the different sponsors, the reform bills through the House. I especially wanted to introduce and coordinate the Open Records Legislation, considered the most important of all the bills. I wanted control of that particular legislation because I knew we would confront considerable opposition. It would be the first attempt to consolidate, under one law, how public records would be made available to the public. In the past, all the governmental bodies and agencies had set their own rules and opposed our efforts at uniformity. Because of the overwhelming opposition we would receive, I felt I was the best of the members to take on that fight and win. I had one of the best legislative assistants, Bill Aleshire, who helped write the bill. He would later be elected Travis County Judge and is recognized as an expert on public records.

My bill was only one in the package of reform bills up for consideration. Early in the session, it became clear that if we were serious about reform, we had to get the entire reform package passed.

Lane Denton & "The Dirty Thirty"

My amendment to the school finance bill would have resulted in our public schools being the best funded in the nation. The school children of Texas lost by two votes.

HB 946—(Consideration continued)

Mr. Hale and Mr. Kubiak moved to table the Denton amendment.

The vote of the House was taken on the motion to table the Denton amendment and the vote was announced Yeas 69, Nays 66.

A verification of the vote was requested and was granted.

The roll of those voting Yea and Nay was again called and the verified vote resulted as follows:
Record No. 8 (page 3499)   65 Yeas
                            63 Nays
                            22 Not Voting

There were nine in total: six legislative and three procedurals in nature. Speaker Daniel strategized that he would appoint co-sponsors to each of the bills. The two sponsors would be based on their ideological leanings: moderate liberal to conservative. The reform package consisted of the following bills: 1) the ethics bill sponsored by James Nugent of Kerrville and Larry Bales from Austin, 2) the lobby regulation and control, and Daniel chose John Bigham of Belton, who was a veteran Dirty Thirtian and Arthur Temple III of Diboll, elected in 1972 as the sponsors.

The third bill created the Ethics Commission to include campaign finance reporting measures with Ben Bynum of Amarillo and Ms. Chris Miller of Fort Worth leading the charge. The bill was designed to replace an antiquated and unenforceable bill Texas had on the books. Carl Parker sponsored the Open Meetings Bill, which would require all governmental bodies, from the executive branch and state legislature to local school boards, to conduct business in open meetings and required advance notice of such meetings to be posted.

Joining me as co-sponsor of the Open Records Bill was Cam Larry of Barnet and Hawkins Menefee of Houston. The other four bills in the reform package dealt with procedural issues. The first one, sponsored by Fred Head, restricted the power of conference committees. The second, under the leadership of Neil Caldwell and Bill Hollowell, would limit the speaker to one term. Until the short reign of Mutscher, it had been an accepted customary rule for the speaker to serve only one term.

He broke that custom and would have served a third term if not stopped by the Sharpstown Scandal. Price Daniel, Jr., who promised to return to the established custom, felt it was now time to make it a law. The third reform procedural bill sponsored by Joe Allen from

Baytown, if passed, would require all candidates for speaker to report all campaign contributions supporting their candidacy. As part of the reform effort, we believed it appropriate for the public to know where the speaker received his financial support so they would know to whom he was in debt. Bob Hendricks from McKinney sponsored the final of the reform bills. It would prohibit the use of threats and promises of rewards in the speaker's race.

My influence in the House of Representatives was extensive because the speaker recognized that as the leader of the Dirty Thirty, and one of the most outspoken proponents of the reform package, I carried a great deal of weight with the members. I was determined to use that influence for the good of the people, specifically minority communities that were underrepresented in governmental agencies.

In early February, I informed the speaker that I planned to investigate the lack of minority employees working for state agencies. He gave me the green light, and I immediately set up an ad hoc committee. I appointed first-term legislator Eddie Bernice Johnson from Dallas (a successful recruit for the Dirty Thirty) and Chris Miller from Fort Worth as co-chairs. Our goal was to highlight the lack of minority employment throughout the state bureaucracy. We held our hearings in the old Supreme Court Chambers, on the third floor of the Capitol building.

In a little over a month, we called all the state agencies before our committee and forced them to share with us the number of minority employees and the positions they held. If the numbers, as it turned out to be the case, were extremely low, we asked for an explanation for their failure to hire them. The statistics were appalling, and the explanations for their failure to hire were just as appalling. Colonel

Wilson Speir, Head of the Department of Public Safety, had to admit there were no Black state troopers or Texas Rangers, only janitors.

Without giving us the truth for the failure, we knew all along the reason. The Department, undoubtedly supported by the governor, did not want a situation where a Black state trooper could stop a White man, woman, or family on the highways of Texas. It allowed a Black too much power over a White, and even in 1973, Texas was not quite ready for that kind of situation.

Representative Eddie B. Johnson, Ms. Chris Miller, and Lane Denton asking questions about the employment statistics of state agencies. Today, Representative Johnson is chair of the powerful House Committee on Science, Space, and Technology. She is a dear friend and endorsed me in every race. Representative Johnson was born in Waco, Texas, and her parents were my constituents.

Lane Denton & "The Dirty Thirty"

Representative Paul Ragsdale continued the employment study. Representative Ragsdale served seven outstanding terms. He was endorsed by the Dirty Thirty in 1972. Paul was an all-state saxophone player in high school. At the University of Texas, he was not allowed to join the Longhorn marching band because he was Black. Paul continued the employment issues after he left the Legislature. He was an outstanding member of the Texas House of Representatives.

The rest of the agencies fared no better. I found the situation quite disgusting, as did Eddie Bernice Johnson. She let them know exactly how she felt, and her expression of disgust did not sit well with Robert Calvert, State Comptroller. Right outside the old Supreme Courtroom in front of the press, he referred to Johnson as that "nigger woman." That comment led to his downfall. The next year he did not run for reelection. Even Conservative Texas would not tolerate that kind of insult perpetrated against an elected official.

Our ad hoc committee hearings did not result in any legislation. But the press had followed them closely and ultimately led to changes in the hiring practices in state agencies. To that end, our hearing was a success, but also put a target on me by the powers to be in the state.

The first of the reform bills to come to the house floor for a final vote was the conference committee limitation bill. Overwhelmingly passed with little opposition, Daniel was able to send it over to the Senate with no amendments. The next bill to be considered was the open meetings, and it attracted some opposition. Some members complained their constituents expressed concern as to the extent of intrusion into their lives the bill would cause. For example, would a conversation over lunch with only two elected officials be subject to the open meetings requirement?

Parker accepted an amendment that made such meetings exempt from the law if it did not constitute a quorum of the body. One amendment that Parker adamantly opposed called for criminal penalties for anyone who filed a false complaint under the law. Parker argued on the floor that the amendment, if passed, could be used as a tool of intimidation against citizens wanting to file complaints. However, the amendment passed on a 72-71 vote.

My bill finally came to the House floor on February 13. Our only serious opposition came from Representative E. L. Short. He offered an amendment, if passed, would have made open records optional to all the public agencies under its reach. We defeated his amendment and the open records bill was sent to the Senate for its consideration.

The remainder of the reform bills were progressing with few bumps, and then came the ethics bill. The major stumbling block was an amendment introduced by Fred Angich, a Republican and billionaire, a Dirty Thirty supporter. His amendment called for the public financial disclosure requirement for all public officials, subject to its jurisdiction to be filed in a sealed envelope, subject to being opened by the Ethics Commission based on probable cause, as a result of an investigation or a complaint.

Debate on the House floor became quite heated. Hawkins Menefee claimed that the amendment "would deliver a crippling blow to the reform movement." Both Nugent and Bales, the two sponsors, adamantly opposed the amendment, but it still passed on a 71-70 vote. However, it was ultimately removed. Daniel, who also voted against the amendment, made one of his rare speeches when he proclaimed, "I am very, very disappointed. I don't think the House acted in accordance with the mandate of the people as expressed in last year's election." With the last of the reform bills finally passed, they then made their way over to the Senate.

We knew the entire reform package would face a great deal of opposition on the other side of the Capitol. There had been quite a turnover in the Senate. Fifteen of the thirty-one members were new, and to make matters worse, eight of the fifteen were former members of the House and had been loyal to Mutscher. We assumed they would not be strong advocates for the reform movement. Also, the Senate had always been a conservative body, reluctant to accept change to the status quo. I felt there was a possibility that we could lose all the reform bills in the Senate. My concern was that our bills passed in the House would be altered in the Senate and forced to the conference committee, and there they would die because time would run out.

The first of the reform bills to be taken up in the Senate, House Bill 5, the Conference Committee Limitation Bill, came up for a vote on the Senate floor on March 21. After very little debate and to our surprise, the bill was defeated on a 21-10 vote. Daniel told the press that the defeat of what could be considered the least controversial bill was a stunning blow. We now knew we had to dig in our heels and prepare for a real battle for the next one hundred days.

During the first week of April, we experienced our first victory as the Senate passed the Open Meetings Bill, but not without some changes. The most important change was that they added an amendment exempting meetings of public officials at social functions or government-sponsored workshops. Parker convinced us to go along with the change. We did, and the bill was sent to Governor Dolph Briscoe for his signature.

To our complete satisfaction, the Senate passed House Bills 8 and 9, and both were signed by the governor. However, it did not take long for our confidence to be somewhat shattered when Attorney General John Hill, at the request of Senator William T. (Bill) Moore, ruled House Bill Number 7 unconstitutional. Even though most of the House members felt it was good for the body of the House to restrict a speaker to one term, after our struggles and problems with Mutscher, that bill went up in smoke thanks to the attorney general.

Entering the last month of the legislative session, the scorecard read that of the nine reform bills, three had passed and two had failed. We still had four more to go, so we dug in, determined not to lose another to the Senate.

Finally, on May 17, with only two weeks left in the session, my open records bill passed on the Senate side, but not without some struggle. The bill passed in the House back in February and was sent to the Senate. It did not come to the Senate floor until the middle of May. The problem lay with Senator Charles Herring from Austin. He was heavily under the influence of all the state agencies in his senatorial district. They did not want the bill to pass. Herring was also the attorney for the Lower Colorado Authority, and they also opposed the bill. Herring stalled for as long as he possibly could. I went to Hobby and told him we needed to pass the remaining reform bills without any further delay. I subtly reminded him that his past problems might resurface if he did not get the open records bill as well as the remaining reform legislation passed on the Senate floor.

Only a few days later, the Open Records Bill was voted on with some changes. I extensively studied the changes made but concluded they did not hurt the bill. Some of the House members wanted to take it to a conference, but I knew that late in the session, it would never get a final vote. If the bill went back to the Senate, and then to a conference committee, it would likely die. I met with the speaker and his assistant, Carlton Carl, and Bill Aleshire, and we all agreed we should pass the bill as it came out of the Senate.

I rose on the House floor and delivered a convincing speech that we pass the bill as is. In many ways, the Open Records Bill was the foundation for all the reform and what it would mean for the state. The speaker agreed, and with his support, the bill passed in the House and was sent to the governor for his signature.

The Open Records we passed has been considered the best in the nation, and the University of Missouri Freedom Information Center has recognized it as the absolute best, and it was used as a model by legislatures all over the country. It has held the test of time and is just one of the great reform bills to pass through the 63rd Legislative Session.

With only five days left, we still had three reform bills left to pass. The most critical of the three was the ethics bill. When it was reported out of the Jurisprudence Committee on the Senate side, it had been considerably altered. The attitude of Senator Herring reflected the changes. He had made it quite clear that he believed public officials were basically honest and, therefore, should not be presumed to be dishonest. When the revised Senate version came back to the House floor, Nugent urged all members to reject the bill and send it to the conference committee. Now I began to worry because three reform bills, ethics, campaign contributions, and lobby control were still lingering. After considerable back-and-forth wrangling, the first of the three campaign contributions was resolved and approved by both the Senate and House.

By Saturday, with only two days left in the session, the acrimony continued. We got word that Senator Moore went into a tirade against the ethics bill, the speaker, and, in fact, against the entire reform movement. After putting up with his temper tantrum late Saturday night, the conferees finally agreed on a compromised version of the bill, and it was sent back to the House and Senate for a final vote. I breathed a sigh of relief. Now two down and one to go.

That one was the lobby bill, and as of Monday morning, it was still in a stalemate in the conference committee. The lobbyists were busy trying to influence conference committee members, and it caused a rather disorderly and chaotic scene right outside the committee room. The entire House membership sat on the House floor, waiting nervously to see if we would vote on all three of the bills before midnight. Finally, at 9:00 p.m., with only three hours left in the 63rd Legislative session, we were presented with all three of the bills and approved them in both the Senate and the House. At midnight, we all cheered. What we had set out to do back in January, we achieved. Without a doubt, our legislative session, known as the Reform Legislature, will go down as the greatest and most successful legislative session in history. Credit goes to Speaker Price Daniel and his administrative assistant, Carlton Carl, and the Dirty Thirty members.

Lane Denton

May 11, 1973   HOUSE JOURNAL   3499

DOROTHY HALLMAN
Chief Clerk

JEANETTE BURK
Journal Clerk

63RD LEGISLATURE
STATE OF TEXAS
HOUSE OF REPRESENTATIVES
PRICE DANIEL, JR., Speaker
REGULAR SESSION

RECORD NO. **8**
VERIFIED

SUMMARY				DATE 5-11-73
YEA	NAY	PRESENT—Not Voting	ABSENT	
065	063	001	02	

MEMORANDA
—Member absent
X—Member absent-excused MOTION TO TABLE DENTON AMENDMENT TO COMMITTEE AMENDMENT #1, HB 946
C—Member in the Chair

106

Lane Denton & "The Dirty Thirty"

News-Tribune
Waco, Texas

JUN 14 1973

Briscoe Inks 2 Bills in Waco

Gov. Dolph Briscoe signed two legislative bills in Waco Wednesday. Both were authored by Rep. Lane Denton.

The first bill signed relates to autistic children who previously were not covered under the Mental Health-Mental Retardation Program. These are children with special handicaps. The bill provides for inclusion of these children in the state's special education programs to handle their problems.

The other bill gives cities the opportunity to offer reduced transit fares to those 60 years and older.

Both measures will go into effect Sept. 1.

I asked two Young Democrats from Baylor University to join me at the signing ceremony. As a courtesy, I asked my fellow House member from Waco, Texas, Lyndon Olson, Jr., to also joined me.

This photo made the front page of all daily newspapers, thanks to the excellent photographer, Kurt Wallace.

Lane Denton

Page 4, Section 1 ☆☆ Houston Chronicle Thursday, January 13, 1977

Photo by E. Joseph Deering, Chronicle Staff

Sitting in for Daddy

Dee Ann Denton, 7-year-old daughter of state Rep. Lane Denton of Waco, sits at her father's desk in the House Chamber Wednesday. (Related stories, picture on Page 8, Section 1.)

4.

With the most successful legislative session in the history of the Texas State Legislature, one in which I played a critical role, now over, I returned to Waco and considered my future. Congressman Poage, who represented my district, had been in office for over thirty-seven years, and we all knew that soon he would retire. There were rumblings in the House of Representatives that the Democratic Caucus considered removing men like Poage from chairmanship positions because they were too conservative. If he were forced out as chairman of the Agriculture Committee, I knew he would probably retire, and I contemplated a run for his seat when that happened. I also prepared for the Constitutional Convention scheduled for January 1974.

I hadn't been back to Austin in a couple of months, but that would abruptly change when it was reported in the news that a young girl had mysteriously died in a childcare facility in Liberty, Texas, and there had been no investigation by the Department of Public Welfare as to the cause of her death. The facility was allowed to stay open, and the license was revoked. What came with the most successful legislative session in the history of the Texas State Legislature, one in which I played a critical role, now over, I returned to Waco and considered my future. Congressman Poage, who represented my district, had been in office for over thirty-seven years, and we all knew that soon he would retire. There were rumblings in the House of Representatives that the Democratic Caucus considered removing men like Poage from chairmanship positions because they were too conservative. If he were forced out as chairman of the Agriculture Committee, I knew he would probably retire, and I contemplated a run for his seat when that happened. I also prepared for the Constitutional Convention scheduled for January 1974.

I hadn't been back to Austin in a couple of months, but that would abruptly change when it was reported in the news that a young girl had mysteriously died in a childcare facility in Liberty, Texas, and there had been no investigation by the Department of Public Welfare as to the cause of her death. The facility was allowed to stay open, and the license was revoked. What came to light and was revealed by the press was that Price Daniel, Jr., was the attorney for the facility. With extreme pressure on the speaker, he called for an investigation of the facility by the subcommittee of the Public Welfare Committee that I chaired.

Due to the many changes implemented during the 1973 legislative session, we had much more power than ad hoc investigative committees in the past, and that would work to my benefit. To begin with, we had paid staff to work on the investigation and we had the authority to subpoena witnesses to testify. And in this case, we had strong support from the press. However, there was one major problem confronting us. Since the speaker was also the attorney for the facility, the assumption was that it had escaped any sanctions because of his involvement. In a very precarious position, we had to

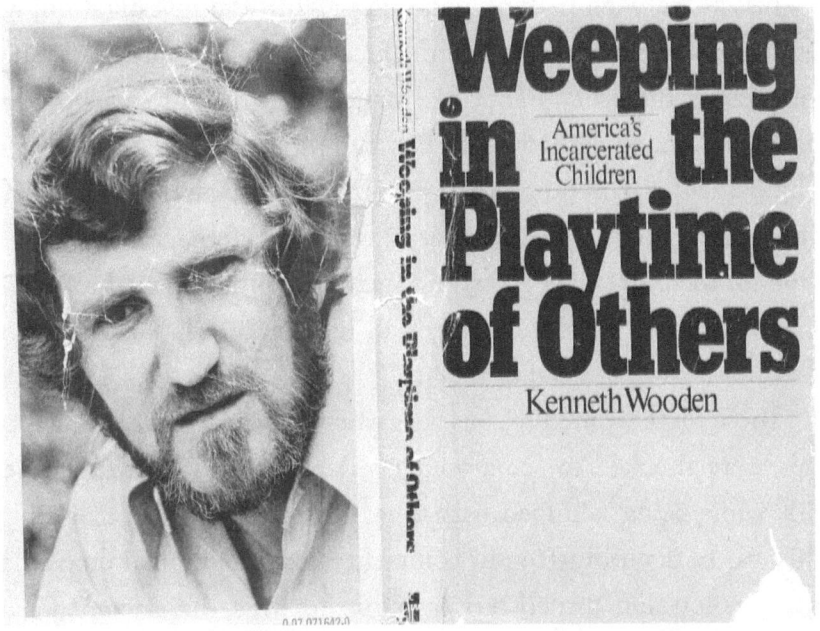

Kenneth Wooden's award-winning book provided the details of the Texas child care scandals.

determine if the speaker exercised his influence within the state to keep the school open.

What furthermore made our position rather precarious was that Lieutenant Governor William Hobby insisted the investigation be conducted thoroughly. I questioned Hobby's motivation. He knew Daniel had served one term as speaker and would now target new positions to seek, including lieutenant governor, attorney general, or even governor. These were the positions coveted by Hobby for the future. What more effective way to eliminate a strong opponent than through a good scandal? Hobby was quite pleased when we began the investigation.

Just as we were making good progress in the investigation, we received an unexpected visit from three mothers. What they shared with us was disturbing. They had visited their daughters, who were locked up in a rehabilitation facility run by Reverend Lester Roloff, a fundamentalist Baptist preacher who owned Roloff Evangelistic Enterprises. He was the founder of Rebekah Home, established in 1968 for the purpose of providing shelter for girls addicted to drugs, prostitutes, girls who had served jail time, and girls kicked out of their homes and in need of refuge.

These three women told us that when they arrived at the facility, they were shocked to see a young girl being held down by other girls while being whipped with what appeared to be a razor strap. This was so disturbing to our committee that we stopped our initial investigation and turned our attention to what these women had reported to us. What we uncovered was more than disturbing. It was horrific. Reverend Roloff first began bringing young girls to the Rebekah Home for Girls in 1968. The Rebekah Home was run from a biblical perspective, Proverbs, which reads, "Withhold not correction from the child: for if thou beatest him with the rod, he shall not die." Roloff carried that dictum to the extreme. The girls were not allowed to watch television or listen to the radio, except for only one hour per day, and that was to listen to Roloff's sermon. They had to attend church services daily. The windows were locked all the time with no rear door, and the facility had an alarm system to prevent the girls from escaping. Parents were allowed only limited visits, and there had to be some mistake that these three ladies witnessed the whipping.

When we summoned Reverend Roloff before our committee and confronted him with the affidavits of sixteen young girls who had been locked up at Rebekah facilities, he responded by telling the committee that his method of punishment was "good old-fashioned discipline, solidly supported by Scripture." He told the committee, "Better a pink bottom than a black soul."

We insisted his homes come under the oversight of the Public Welfare Agency and he argued that his was a religious home and organization and therefore exempt from state interference in his operation. Having done as much as we could as a legislative body out of session, we asked Attorney General John Hill to act against Roloff, and his efforts eventually led to the closing of the Rebeka School. Legal battles with Roloff continued until 1985, when finally, all his schools were forced to close.

A young observer, Karl Rove, of Roloff and his use of religion as a political tool, recognized how useful this approach could be in the future. In the 1978 gubernatorial election, he used Roloff and his tremendous influence with all the religious churches and groups in Texas to help defeat Democrat John Hill for governor. Years later, he would use the same approach to elevate George W. Bush to Governor of the state and eventually President of the United States.

Our investigation into Artesia Hall continued, and eventually we forced it to close. But then another crisis appeared when I received a lead from an *Austin-American-Statesman* newspaper reporter. The reporter told me of the Mary Lee School, located fifty miles west of Austin, and its abusive treatment of young Black girls brought there for confinement from Chicago, Illinois. I convinced Representative Ben Reyes from Austin to join me on a surprise visit trip to the facility.

When we arrived there, we were in awe of the situation before us. The girls were confined to unhealthy, dirty cages, like those for animals, as their living quarters. There had to be over two hundred girls piled into those cages. The girls had been sent to the Mary Lee facility instead of going to reform prisons in Chicago. They lived in those cages just like animals. They were all seriously overweight. We discovered that the facility received funds from the Upjohn Company and that the girls were being used as guinea pigs to research Depo-Provera, a drug that could prevent pregnancy. One of the side effects was weight gain.

It was a deplorable sight and situation. No human being should be subjected to such cruel and unusual punishment, especially young girls who still had their entire lives before them. I was irate and embarrassed that my state would allow such cruelty toward other human beings in all three cases we investigated. The May Lee facility closed, and all the girls were sent back to Chicago. The story was covered in news stories on NBC News, Chicago's daily papers, and *Reader's Digest* in March 1976.

I considered these investigations an extension of what the reform movement in the legislature was all about. The people in Texas were not in the mood to tolerate any kind of abuse, be it political, economic, or social. They were calling for reform and that carried over to the Texas Constitution as it also came under attack.

Lane Denton & "The Dirty Thirty"

My appointment as Chair of House Public Welfare Subcommittee with Speaker Price Daniel, Jr., and Representative Carlos Truan.

At a press conference presenting the committee's report.

Lane Denton

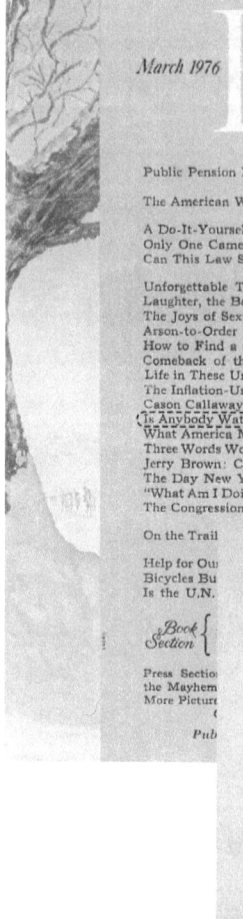

The article in *Reader's Digest* gave my subcommittee hundreds of investigation tips.

Lane Denton & "The Dirty Thirty"

Representative Ben Reyes, a Vietnam Veteran that the Dirty Thirty endorsed. He helped with my child care investigation. He was a hardworking and excellent legislator.

REPS. LANE DENTON, LEFT, OF WACO, AND BEN REYES OF HOUSTON
Look Over Wire Cage at The Mary Lee School South of Austin

Lane Denton Introduces Four Bills

News-Tribune Austin Bureau

AUSTIN — Waco Reprersentative Lane Denton Thursday introduced four bills i nthe house of representatives — one of which will exempt 15-year-olds enrolled in a technical-vocational education program orwork-study program from the compulsory attendance law.

The exemption requires approval by the principal, at least two teachers and the counselor of the public school the student would otherwise attend. Approval of the parent or guardian must also be granted.

At present the compulsory attendance law applies to all children through age of 17.

Other bills introduced by Denton would:

—Include retarded and emotionally disturbed (autistic) children under the definition of "exceptional children" eligible for special instruction. Denton said existing legislation provides aid for the retarded and also for emotionally disturbed, but children with both handicaps have' been bypassed. In Denton's bill, autistic includes children who are physically handicapped, retarded and emotionally disturbed.

— Permitting firemen and policemen to live outside the limits of the city or town that employs them.

—Allowing firemen suffering disablement or death from heart or lung disease as a consequence of duties as a fireman to receive pension benefits from the city.

The bill is an amendment to legislation passed during the last regular session which gives cities the option of offering benefits.

5.

On January 8, 1974, Lieutenant Governor William Hobby made history when he gaveled in the opening of the Texas Constitutional Convention. The last convention to change the state's constitution occurred in 1876. As a result, many citizens complained it had become an anachronism unfit for contemporary Texas. It had been written to replace the Constitution of 1869, known as the Reconstruction Constitution. The 1869 Constitution had taken all the power from the establishment (slavocracy) and given it to those who had opposed the civil war and what was considered the interlopers from the north coming south to gain power. It was also given to ex-slaves, allowing them to vote. All the power was centralized in Republican Governor E.J. Davis. However, once the Union Army left Texas in 1876, as a result of the presidential compromise and the election of Rutherford B. Hayes, power was returned to the old guard, and the business, economic, and political elite gathered and wrote the Constitution of 1876. It was written to favor their interests, and remained that way with little change.

The effort for change began as early as 1970, when the League of Women Voters and Common Cause raised the issue. One of their goals was to reduce the constitution from eighty-nine thousand words to something more manageable. It was compared to the United States Constitution, which is only seven thousand two hundred words, and applies to all fifty states, and has been effective since 1789. Another goal was to require the state legislature to meet year-round and every year, instead of the one hundred eighty days in odd numbered years. The business community, especially the banking industry, supported the call for a convention. The business community's motivation was to get the right to work incorporated into a new constitution. It was now law, but according to the business community, instead of being a statue that could easily be changed, they wanted it ensconced in the constitution, and only an amendment (much more difficult to get) could eradicate it. The banking community's motivation was to change the rules of taxation for the purposes of taking property from someone who failed to pay a loan. They wanted the definition of property to include much more than just a debtor's home, but also personal items such as jewelry that had some value.

My reason for supporting the convention was to achieve, through a new constitution, what I had failed to get done legislatively. I saw this as an opportunity to equalize the proportion of resources distributed among school districts throughout the states. It was also an opportunity to increase the resources available to the districts by expanding the definition of property beyond just the home.

During the 1971 legislative session, we had approved a resolution to be sent to voters in the 1972 election for their approval to convene the convention in January 1974. The voters gave their approval by a resounding 1,549,982 votes. The next step in the process was to appoint a thirty-seven-member Constitutional Revision Commission. It was their responsibility, after holding nineteen public hearings throughout the state, to draw up a new constitution as a document for discussion during the convention. The Commission was to be appointed by the governor, lieutenant governor, speaker of the house, chief justice of the Supreme Court, and the presiding judge of the Court of Criminal Appeals.

I was disappointed when the list of chosen members for the Commission was revealed. It was not a cross-section of citizens of the state but instead businessmen, financiers, bankers, and farm bureau representatives, a very conservative group not seriously in favor of change except for that change that benefitted them. The only acceptable representative on the Commission, from my perspective, was former United States Senator Ralph Yarborough, who managed through his very persuasive skills, to do a good job in trying to make the others come to grips with some real problems facing the state that needed to be addressed and not changes that would simply line their pockets with more of the state's resources. If I had overseen picking the Commission, I would have appointed those men and women that I genuinely believed were capable, intelligent, and independent in their thinking and whom the business elite could not control.

The Commission worked from March 28 to September 23 under the leadership of Chief Justice of the Supreme Court Robert Calvert and Mrs. Beryl Millburn as chair and co-chair. Justice Calvert had a very distinguished record steeped deeply in Texas politics. He was elected to the Texas Legislature in 1932 and became Speaker of the House of Representatives from 1937 to 1939. He was on the Executive Committee of the Democratic State Party from 1946 to 1948, first elected as an Associate Justice of the Supreme Court in 1950 and elevated to Chief Justice in 1961, and served in that capacity until 1972. He was a very distinguished jurist, and no one had problems, including me, with his appointment as chair of the Commission.

Delegates to the convention were the one hundred eighty-one members of the Texas State Legislature. That caused some problems with the League of Women Voters, who believed the delegates selected should have been from the general population. But they lost that battle as a compromise to get the 1971 Legislature to approve the resolution to go to the voters. On the second day of the convention, Price Daniel, Jr., was sworn in as president, and I supported his nomination for that position. Having him in charge meant that the leader was a friend to the Dirty Thirty and leaned liberal on most of the issues to be taken up at the convention.

Once we got started, I was convinced that the new constitution would never make its way out of the convention to the voters for their approval. There was just too much conflict among the different factions fighting for their proposals to be the ones adopted. Lobbyists were all over the place from day one, pushing for their programs. And also, the League of Women Voters, as well as Common Cause, seemed to have disappeared once the convention began and were not highly active in fighting for their choice issues. We were depending on them for support of the more liberal issues. We also took several breaks during the seven-month period.

On March 13, Delegate Hawkins Menefee was killed in an automobile accident coming back from Houston, where he had met with his constituents. Hawkins had been a strong supporter of the convention, and just before he left to go home that fatal weekend, he had attacked the press for their tendency to concentrate on the negative aspects of the convention. He exclaimed to the press that most of the delegates were dedicated, hardworking members, but the press only wanted to concentrate on what he termed the "goof-offs."

The convention was suspended for three days, and Southwest Airlines provided an airplane to fly all one hundred eighty-one members to Dallas to attend Hawkins' memorial service. We also took a week off in April to return to our districts and campaign. After all, there was an election coming up in November and some members were facing stiff competition. I had minimum competition from a candidate put up by the Chamber of Commerce. However, I still returned to the district and put in some work with my constituents. My thoughts were on the congressional seat in the future.

President of the Convention, Price Daniel, was determined to keep criticism of the proceedings to a minimum. Even though several amendments resonated well with the League and with Common Cause, they refused to go public. The two lobbyists for Common Cause, Buck Wood and Randall Wood, were close friends of Daniel. They did not want to do anything to cause criticism of the convention that could be interpreted as criticisms of him because they knew it might hurt his future plans to run for a higher office.

The final document offered to the delegates was intensely debated for two days and finally failed to pass by two votes. I voted against it because it was designed to serve the interests of the elite, and, even though we had gotten a section to improve the financing of the school districts, it just was not enough. Half the members voted for it, regardless of how bad it was, simply because they wanted to be recorded in history as one of one hundred eighty-one who approved a new constitution for the state. However, I strongly believed there must be some decency and pride in doing the right thing, and voting in favor of that very flawed constitution was not the right thing to do.

I returned to Waco and, with only four months to the election, met with my constituents. I had been gone for seven months in an election year, which is never a good thing for a candidate, no matter how secure they are in their district. The Republicans offered only token opposition, but still, as an astute politician, I knew better than to take anything for granted.

I easily won reelection to my third term in the Texas State Legislature with an overwhelming vote. I would now return to Austin as an established leader of the Dirty Thirty with a great track record of getting things done in the legislature. I looked forward to the upcoming session and all that we could continue to accomplish for the people of Texas.

Lane Denton & "The Dirty Thirty"

Behind me is my legislative assistant, Roy Walthal, who did an outstanding job and is now recognized as a leader for constitutional reform.

Looking over an amendment by San Antonio Delegate Nelson Wolff. Delegate Wolff and I generally voted on opposite sides.

Addressing the convention on the urgent need for equitable funding for our public schools.

Lane Denton

Addressing the convention to support keeping the homestead provision in the constitution. Mortgage companies and banks wanted to remove the provision.

WACO LABOR JOURNAL

This Paper has the Official Endorsement of The McLennan County Central Labor Council

WACO, TEXAS, FRIDAY, JULY 25, 1975

CAPITOL REPORT
from Lane Denton

Last week I released a report from my office showing that the Central Intelligence Agency has at times secretly funded a research project at a state mental health institution in Houston since 1964. I found that the Texas Research Institute of Mental Sciences (TRIMS), which is an institution under the Texas MHMR Department, has received over $126,000 to conduct research for the CIA in perfecting the reliability of lie detector machines.

I have said that I find no serious objection to law enforcement agencies or national security agencies improving the reliability of lie detector machines, if appropriate safeguards are set on to insure that such super-detection devices are not misused. But I do strongly object to having an agency of the State of Texas, such as TRIMS, misused and misdirected by the CIA.

TRIMS was established by the Texas Legislature and assigned the task of conducting research relevant to "treating mental illness." In the research materials of the lie detector tests at TRIMS, there is no mention of the value or benefit this research would have to treating mental illness. The researchers at TRIMS did not apply for funds from mental health agencies for this study and have not continued their work in perfecting the polygraph.

TRIMS is supposed to be doing research designed to treat and prevent mental illness. They could serve a very important function in reducing the incidence of mental illness in our state, and this is one of the reasons I am very concerned that so much time and energy has been spent on the CIA project. The taxpayers of Texas spend almost $200 million per year to help treat 18,000 Texans who are mentally-ill or mentally-retarded. TRIMS could have a positive impact on reducing this caseload, and I am hopeful more effort will be made in this area.

I have forwarded the results of my investigation of the CIA involvement to Senator Frank Church, Chairman of the U. S. Senate Committee on the CIA Investigation. I asked Senator Church to include, as part of his investigation, the domestic involvement of the CIA in other State or local non-law enforcement agencies, such as TRIMS.

I also discovered in this investigation, that the CIA had funded part of this research indirectly through a private corporation in California and also through the U. S. Air Force. When the State MHMR Board met to consider whether or not to accept contracts with the California corporation or the Air Force, the Board members were not informed that these were actually CIA projects. It seems to me to be a very serious matter when a Federal agency, such as the CIA, deliberately misleads our state officials, who have the right and the responsibility to control the activities of our state agencies.

I am hopeful and confident that positive benefit to our state and to our nation will come from these revelations. I believe it will encourage our state officials to become more familiar with the actual workings of all our State agencies, and that can't hurt.

> Bernard Rapport and I had the opportunity to have a long visit with Senator Frank, Church. Senator Church said the CIA is one of most the dangerous organizations in the world.

Serving with Delegate Fred Agnich on The Finance Committee.

Talking with fellow delegates about the strategy to keep "Right to Work" out of the document. This was the major reason the newly proposed constitution was defeated.

Lane Denton & "The Dirty Thirty"

LANE DENTON
P. O. BOX 3204
MCCLENNAN COUNTY
WACO, TEXAS 76707

State of Texas
House of Representatives
Austin

Mr. Clyde Whiteside, Chairman
Texas Board of Pardons and Paroles
Stephen F. Austin State Office Building, Room 711
Austin, Texas 78701

Dear Mr. Whiteside:

After reviewing the case of inmate ███████████, ██████, and his adjustment within the Department of Corrections, I am sending you this letter to serve as my recommendation that his sentence of 40 years for the sale of marijuana be reduced to 15 years.

My reasons for making this recommendation are as follows: proof that ██████ adjustment within the TDC has been a productive one is provided by the facts that (1) he is a state approved trustee, (2) he has accrued 225 points on his incentive program, and (3) he has participated in many rehabilitative projects including the educational program, alcoholics anonymous, and the sports program.

Thank you for your consideration.

Sincerely,

Lane Denton
Lane Denton
LD/js

cc: ███████████

> *Note: There are people still in prison today from sentencing in the 1970s to the 1980s. Therefore, the election of the governor is important.*

PENALTY FOR SIMPLE POSSESSION OF MARIJUANA (FIRST OFFENSE)

State	Penalty	State	Penalty
ALABAMA	5–20 years and may be fined up to $20,000	MONTANA	Up to 5 years in the state pris...
ALASKA	Up to 1 year and/or up to $1000	NEBRASKA	7 days in jail and the offen... complete an educative cours... (for possession of less than 8 ... less than 25 marijuana cigarett...
ARIZONA	Up to 1 year in the county jail or up to $1000 or 1 to 10 years in the state prison, at the discretion of the court	NEVADA	1–6 years and up to $2000
ARKANSAS	2–5 years and up to $2000	NEW HAMPSHIRE	Up to 1 year and/or up to $... possession of less than 1 poun...
CALIFORNIA	1–10 years in the state prison or up to 1 year in the county jail	NEW JERSEY	2–15 years and up to $2000
COLORADO		SOUTH DAKOTA	Up to 1 year and/or up to $$ possession of 1 ounce or less)
LOUISIANA	1 year and/or $500		
MAINE	Up to 11 months and up to $1000	TENNESSEE	2–5 years and up to $500
MARYLAND	2–5 years and up to $1000	TEXAS	2 years to life
MASSACHUSETTS	Up to 2½ years in jail or house of correction or up to 3½ years in the state prison or up to $1000	UTAH	Not less than 6 months
		VERMONT	Up to 6 months and/or up to $...
MICHIGAN	Up to 10 years and up to $5000	VIRGINIA	Up to 12 months and/or up to ...
MINNESOTA	5–20 years and up to $10,000	WASHINGTON	Up to 6 months and/or up to $...
MISSISSIPPI	2–5 years and up to $2000	WEST VIRGINIA	2–5 years and up to $1000
MISSOURI	6 months to 1 year in the county jail or up to 20 years in the state correctional institution, at the discretion of the court	WISCONSIN	Up to 1 year and/or up to $500
		WYOMING	Up to 6 months in jail and up to ...

6.

With the retirement of Price Daniel, Jr., the first order of business for the 1975 64th Legislative Session was the selection of a new speaker of the House. With my urging of Representative Fred Head, the Dirty Thirty threw their support behind Bill Clayton, first elected to the House in 1962 from Spring Lake in West Texas. We had some concerns because he was a conservative, but supported many of our reforms in the prior legislative session. I believed he would continue the procedural

Accepting the Social Services Committee Chairmanship from Speaker Bill Clayton.

Presenting information to my committee about the urgent need for community mental health services.

reforms that we had initiated in 1973 and work to make them even stronger. Speaker Clayton appointed me Chairman of the House Social Services Committee, which had jurisdiction over many of the state agencies to include the Department of Welfare, the Texas Prison System, the Health Agencies, School for the Deaf and Blind, and Mental Health and Mental Retardation Agencies. This Committee was a great fit for me because of my extreme interest in improving the quality of life for those with the least influence on their government.

Being the chair of the Committee allowed me to hire sufficient staff, something lacking when I was simply a member of the legislature. I hired Margaret Moore, the daughter of Tom Moore, whom I had known for an awfully long time, as my general counsel for the Committee. She was elected Travis County District Attorney in 2019. Besides Margaret, I hired Jim Phillips, who is now legal counsel at The University of Texas at Austin. Bill Aleshire was my administrative assistant, and he later became a Travis County Judge. So, I had an outstanding staff working for me in Austin and they made a tremendous difference in a lot of my activities during and after the 1975 legislative session. Back in Waco, I had two young staffers, Hope Dominquez and Barry Bryant, one Hispanic and a young Black student at Baylor. Two additional staffers, Jack Holcomb and Joel Smith, gave me an outstanding staff. They took good care of my constituents back in Waco while I was at the Capitol.

One of House Speaker Clayton's major goals was to place a greater emphasis on expanding the roles of the legislative standing committees. He encouraged the committee chairmen to conduct research on legislative issues during the session and after it ended in May. That opened the door for me to get involved in several issues I found quite disturbing. An area of concern for me was the many people that were imposed for minor crimes. I was determined to attack that problem but ran into great opposition from my co-chair of the Committee, Representative Jimmie Edwards. He represented Huntsville, the location of the major prison facility in Texas. His constituents in that community opposed any changes to the existing rules on the books for an exceedingly long time.

One of my first committee hearings took on unfair sentencing of prisoners based on race. I had W.J. Estelle, Director of the Texas Prison System, before the Committee. In his testimony, he told the

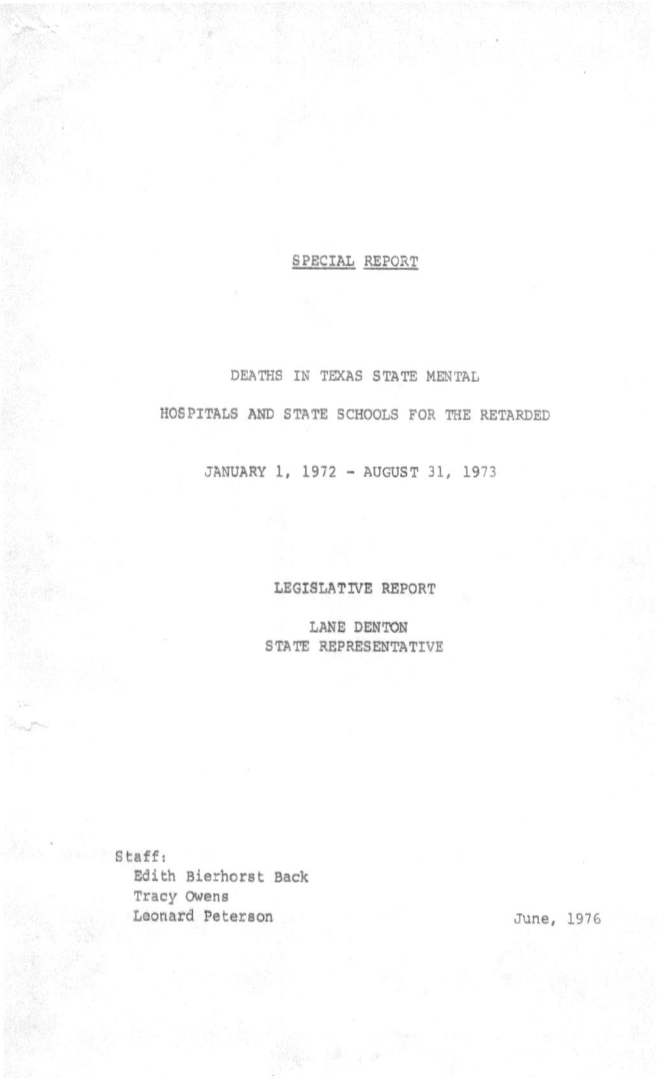

SPECIAL REPORT

DEATHS IN TEXAS STATE MENTAL
HOSPITALS AND STATE SCHOOLS FOR THE RETARDED

JANUARY 1, 1972 - AUGUST 31, 1973

LEGISLATIVE REPORT

LANE DENTON
STATE REPRESENTATIVE

Staff:
 Edith Bierhorst Back
 Tracy Owens
 Leonard Peterson   June, 1976

Along with excellent staff, I authored a landmark study that has had a major impact on our treatment of individuals with special health needs.

Lane Denton

NE DENTON
. O. BOX 3204
ENNAN COUNTY
O, TEXAS 76707

State of Texas
House of Representatives
Austin

P. O. BOX 2910
CAPITOL STATION
AUSTIN, TEXAS

July 1, 1976

    The report which follows is the result of many hours of research and diligent effort by dedicated people. They recognize a problem is developing within our existing system of care for the retarded and that corrective action must be taken. The conclusions drawn as a result of this report are in no way meant to point a finger of blame, but rather to bring to the attention of the general public and members of the Legislature conditions which are already known to dedicated staff people in our state institutions and to loving and concerned parents of the retarded who are residents in these institutions.

    The findings of the study indicate approximately one-third of the residents need to be in state hospitals and schools. The remainder could be released to other community facilities, or to their homes. However, Texas does not at the present time have adequate community facilities to accommodate these people, nor does it have adequately developed programs to aid those families of the retarded who could be returned to their homes. At this time there are simply not enough doctors and nurses, not enough emergency medical programs, not enough effective community programs, not enough money.

    There are long waiting lists for most of the state institutions, yet those who must have the full-time care that is provided by state schools and hospitals cannot be accepted due to over-crowding within these institutions. The solution lies in assuring that our existing facilities are adequately staffed and funded to insure proper treatment, and that developed community programs are also available. It is a commitment we must make.

Sincerely,

Lane Denton

members that 40% of the prisoners probably should not even be in prison. Texas had the worst enforcement laws for drugs, especially marijuana, of any state in the union. An individual could get two years to life for one ounce of marijuana. These sentences were based on two criteria: race and poverty. The wealthy White suspect would get probation for the first offense, but if you were a minority, you were sent to prison.

Despite these terrible discrepancies, I know there was no way the Texas Legislature was going to vote for comprehensive change. But I also knew something had to be done, so I went to the chair of the Board of Pardons and Parole, who was former State Representative Clyde Whiteside. He was considered one of the outstanding legislators. Whiteside represented a conservative Texas district. Maybe there was a chance I could help individuals through his cooperation in reducing sentences. That could be a start.

In my meeting with him, I had with me a letter I had received from a constituent, a young Hispanic who had been sentenced to forty years for first possession of one ounce of marijuana. When he contacted my office, he had already served fifteen years. Whiteside agreed to reduce his sentence to fifteen years, already served, and he was released from prison. That was my success on the individual level that I repeated several times, also successful.

Another successful pursuit occurred when I received a tip from Senator Frank Church's office in Washington, DC. He was in the middle of investigating the CIA on the national level. I had met Senator Church through Bernard Rapoport. I recall meeting with him in the nation's capital, and he told me that the CIA was the most dangerous organization in the country. Bill Aleshire, my administrative assistant, discovered that the CIA was in the process of carrying out an experiment on how to pass lie detector tests. They wanted to keep the research secret, so, through an agreement with the Texas Institute of Mental Science, they used that state facility that just happened to fall under my jurisdiction. When I had all my facts, I released a press statement about the secret project. I added the fact that the Legislature had appropriated state money for the research institute and not the CIA. As a result, they were kicked out of the facility. Once again, I took on the powerful and scored a victory. But no doubt they would, in the future, not forget what I did.

As chairman of the Committee, I also conducted a major investigation of nursing homes, targeting two in Houston. I made a midnight visit and discovered serious violations in the treatment of the patients. When I returned to Austin, I introduced legislation that set up a system that called for financial penalties against those homes failing to uphold decent standards in their facilities. However, the lobbyists for the nursing homes were so powerful, they easily convinced members to vote against my legislation and it went down to defeat.

Another additional concern brought to my attention was the tremendous shortage of doctors in the state. With the assistance of my staff, we discovered that many American students were going to Mexico medical schools. The parents of these students came to Austin, and I met with them in the Capitol. I suggested creating a program called the Fifth Pathway. It would allow the American students to come back into the country and complete their fifth year of study in the state of Texas. They would then be licensed as Texas physicians but would have to commit to spending five years in rural Texas as doctors. The parents supported the program; I was able to get it passed through the House and Senate, and Representative

Lane Denton & "The Dirty Thirty"

Explaining the importance of changing horrible Texas drug laws.

Representative Ron Waters was part of the 1973 new legislature. Ron and I participated in a debate about excessive sentencing relating to marijuana offenses. Representative Waters was one of the youngest legislators ever elected. Yes, he smoked marijuana. Some of the older conservative members were shocked. Representative Waters was an excellent and hardworking Democratic member.

Lane Denton

A major fight to have local committees support young offenders. Unfortunately, this important amendment lost by only two votes. Genevieve Tarlton, Sissy Farenthold's sister, helped draft this proposal.

Lane Denton & "The Dirty Thirty"

My deskmate, Representative Ron Bird, was the best-liked member. He brought his pizza machine to Austin and served many members.

Lane Denton

Lane Denton, Chairman

Jim Kaster, Vice-chairman
Gonzalo Barrientos
Joe C. Hanna
Joe A. Hubenak
Bill Presnal
Arthur (Buddy) Temple

John Wilson, Vice-chairman
Appropriative Matters
Jimmie C. Edwards III
Eddie Bernice Johnson
Calvin Rucker

Jim Phillips
Committee Counsel

P. O. Box 2910
Austin, Texas 78767
(512) 475-3424

house of representatives
Committee on
Social Services

September 22, 1976

The Honorable Bill Clayton
Speaker of the House
House of Representatives

Members of the 64th and 65th Legislatures

We, the members of the Social Services Committee for the House of Representatives, herewith submit the report of our studies and recommendations for use by the 65th Legislature.

Lane Denton, Chairman

Jim Kaster, Vice Chairman

John Wilson, Vice Chairman
Appropriative Matters

Joe C. Hanna

Joe A. Hubenak, Chairman
Rehabilitation Subcommittee

Eddie Bernice Johnson

Arthur (Buddy) Temple, Chairman
Juvenile Corrections Subcommittee

Bill Presnal

Jimmie C. Edwards, III, Chairman
Corrections Subcommittee

Calvin Rucker

Gonzalo Barrientos, Chairman
Spanish-Speaking Elderly
Subcommittee

A special thanks to Margaret Moore, Jim Phillips, and Bill Aleshire, staff members who put together the committee's most important recommendations.

Lane Denton & "The Dirty Thirty"

1975
Denton Offers 2 Measures On Farming

Two bills dealing with farming and corporations have been introduced in the Legislature by State Rep. Lane Denton of Waco. HB1665 prohibits corporate farming in the state and HB 1664 prohibits vertical integration in agriculture by corporations.

"These two bills, if enacted, would protect and promote the most efficient method of production of food and fiber, the family-owned production unit," Jay Naman, Waco, president, Texas Farmers Union, said.

Naman urged consumer groups and agriculture organizations to support the two bills and actively work for their enactment.

Naman said vertical integration by large conglomerates pose a threat to the availability and reasonable prices of food items to the consumer.

"As far as the prohibition against corporations, other than family owner-operated, owning or operating farms, I feel this is ultimately in the best interest of consumers. Family farms and ranchers have consistently proven they are the most efficient and economical means of production," Naman said.

A small number of giant corporations control every link of the food chain. Four companies control as much as 90% of the global grain market. The top four beef packers control 85% of the market.

In 1975, I knew if state legislatures or Congress did not step in, this would be the result.

With the help of the Texas Farmers Union, I took on the powerful corporate farm interests.

I introduced landmark legislation (HB 1665 and HB 1664) prohibiting corporate farming and stopping vertical integrations in agriculture by corporations.

I did an extensive study of the cost of food in Berlin, Germany, and San Antonio, Texas. The result showed the cost to be average 30% higher in San Antonio.

Jay Naman, President of Texas Farmers Union, made the following statement: "These two bills by Representative Denton would protect and promote the most efficient method of production of food and fiber, the family-owned production unit."

"Naman said vertical integration by large conglomerates poses a threat to the availability and reasonable prices of food items to the consumer."

I grew up on a family farm in McLennan County in the 1950s. Farmers would get $0.41 from every dollar for their products. Today, that portion has plummeted to $0.15.

Chemical and seed acquisition and mergers allowed three companies to control two-thirds of the crop seed and nearly 70% of the agricultural chemical markets.

Since 2013, the United States farm income has fallen by more than half and the median farm income continues to fall today. Ten thousand farmers declare bankruptcy each year.

Since 2017, almost 2,000 small dairy farms have gone out of business. My brother, John Denton, has been in the daily business for over 40 years. Today, his son, Steve, operates the family dairy farm. Few people realize the operational cost, long hours, and price makes dairy farms a difficult business.

DeeAnn learned early that making money at the Capital was easy. An easy way to make money for ice cream and her favorite, Coca-Cola.

7.

One of the most important agencies in the state of Texas is the three-member Texas Railroad Commission. Its importance over the years had grown even more critical as issues of the environment also became more important. One of the key responsibilities of the Commission is to regulate the gas and oil companies. For years, I had taken an interest in environmental issues and how the corporate world manipulated those issues to their advantage. With the oil embargo from the Middle East in 1973, it caused a crisis in Texas and consumers caught the brunt of that crisis because of the collusion that existed between the Railroad Commission and the powerful oil and gas forces in the state.

One force was Oscar Wyatt, who owned Coastal State later to be renamed Lavaca. He had entered a long-term contract with cities to deliver gas to the large metropolitan areas in the state. He was to provide them with natural gas that then would be sold to the consumer to heat their homes. The manipulation and abuse of the consumer began when the embargo was imposed, causing the cost of natural gas to increase. Wyatt was hit heavily with the increased costs, and his problem was under his contract. He had a set price by which to sell the gas to metropolitan areas. Because he could not increase his costs, he soon faced serious financial problems where he faced bankruptcy. He could not fulfill his contractual responsibility unless some adjustments were worked out with the municipal governments. In other words, unless he raised his cost to the cities.

Wyatt, however, faced one major hurdle, and that was the contract was still locked into place. Here is where the manipulations began. He approached the three-member Railroad Commissioners, all three of whom he had supported in their run for office. They agreed to allow him to do an automatic pass-through of the increased cost for him to provide his product to the municipalities, who, in turn, passed it through to the consumers. As a result, utility bills skyrocketed by thousands of dollars and there was a statewide outcry.

During the 1975 legislative session, my constituents and others throughout the state recognized me as the man to go to when something was wrong, flooding my office with letters, telegrams and telephone calls. They pleaded with me to do something to make a change. To take on this battle would be an uphill struggle within the legislature. I knew the legislature as well as the governor would do nothing to change the situation. Instead of representing their constituents, they really took care of the interest of large oil and gas companies. Eighty percent of all oil and gas is owned by large corporations and the other twenty percent by individual owners. Those large corporations had made large contributions to many in the legislature and the governor. I knew I could get some support from the other members of the legislature, especially the Dirty Thirty, but not enough to overcome those who were bought and sold by the corporations. Coastal States Company was one of those companies that had the legislature in their back pocket.

Lane Denton

I just could not sit around and let this happen. It's in my blood and I had to do something. I created a Consumer Association that raised money for advertising against Texas Power and Light. We opposed the pass-through in every way possible, and the consumer advocates recognized the need for someone on the Commission who would fight for their interests. The opportunity for me materialized when Ben Ramsey, a longtime commissioner and former lieutenant governor, decided not to seek reelection.

The strategy of the powers to be to never have an open seat election for the Commission, but this time it happened. Usually, the candidate up for reelection (the commissioner's term is for six years) has the support of all the major corporations and has no problem raising money. This time, however, the situation would be different. Because there was no incumbent, an outsider not controlled by the giants and, with the support of the everyday voter, could possibly win. Since Poage evidently was not going to retire from Congress, at least not for another two years, and with the strong encouragement I received from many of the consumer and environmental groups for the people, I retired from the legislature and threw my hat in the ring for the commissioner's position.

On December 1, I announced my candidacy for the open seat on the Texas Railroad Commission before a packed crowd in Austin, Texas. From the late summer of 1975 to that day, I had taken my time to form a very competent team. We knew exactly what our major theme would be: the need to get corruption out of the gas and oil business in Texas and bring honesty to the Texas Railroad Commission. I told the press gathered there that I would "dig out the truth about the financial condition of the petroleum resources of oil and gas companies." Representatives from the Texas AFL-CIO,

Lane Denton & "The Dirty Thirty"

Texas Public Employees Association, Consumer and Environmental organizations, and senior citizens' groups applauded my opening statement. I continued, "If the oil giants have deceived the people and the government, if there really are oil and gas resources which are not available to consumers at reasonable prices because these companies insist on exorbitant profits, then the peoples' government, including the Railroad Commission should move quickly and reasonably to expose these deceptions and protect the consumers from further abuses."

Early in the race, newspapers and political pundits throughout the state predicted that I would be one of the leading contenders. They also recognized Jon Newton, a member of the House of Representatives and the oil industry's hand-picked candidate, as a leading contender. The media's goal was to pit the most consumer-oriented candidate against the conservative candidate most friendly to the big oil interests. They were successful in their goals because our race became the most interesting of all political contests in 1976, including the Ford-Carter Presidential race. There were six other candidates that declared early for the Commissioner's seat: Dave Finney, also a member of the Texas House from Fort Worth and former Railroad Commission Hearing Examiner Walter Wendlandt. They were in the race but offered no competition to the voters who would support me.

However, when Terrence O'Rourke, an attorney from Houston, who had assisted the Dirty Thirty during the 63rd Legislative Session, entered the race, it created a real challenge for me. He had been working in Attorney General John Hill's office in the environmental division and was running as the environmental candidate. Having been on Hill's environmental staff and from Houston, he had lots of contacts and received a significant amount of money from the oil industry. The only reason the industry supported him was to cut into my support because we would be pulling from the same constituency. I am not sure why he took on the challenge of running. He probably thought Sissy Farenthold would throw her support behind him, but he was mistaken. She held a press conference and announced her support for me and her son, George Farenthold, Jr., was on my campaign staff. He could not win, but he could hurt me.

The other two candidates were Jerry Sadler and Woodrow Bean, who was a distant relative of the famous Judge Roy Bean. Sadler had a long history of political involvement in the state. He had served in the state legislature, had been land commissioner, and had run for governor on two different occasions. He would later tell me, after the election was over, that he had gotten into the race because some old friends in Houston, with connections to the oil companies, had given his $25,000. He pocketed the money and never reported it as a campaign contribution. I was not surprised.

During the campaign, I had good support. Bill Starnes, who had a well-known country-western singing group, who produced a record and had been the manager for George Jones and Tammy Wynette, supported me. We traveled to all the small country towns, campaigning together. I also had the support of Texas folk humorist John Henry Faulk, who had a role on the television show, *Hee Haw*. He also made appearances throughout the state. Several local newspapers, the *San Marcos Record* and the *Corpus Christi Caller-Times*, supported my campaign, but none of the larger ones. The large daily newspapers were under the control of the oil magnates and threw their support to Newton. However, I lagged far behind Newton in raising money and, as we all unfortunately know, money is the key to success. I raised

Lane Denton & "The Dirty Thirty"

and spent a little over $300,000, but that was nothing compared to Newton's $800,000 and over 90% came from the oil and gas industry. Money always prevails, and that is the number one reform that must happen and the United States does not deal with it, our democracy is in jeopardy.

I finished third in the race, with Sadler finishing first and Newton in second place, but there had to be a run-off because no one received most of the vote. Newton won the run-off and became the third commissioner of the Railroad Commission. I do believe I really could have won that race if several unfortunate incidents hadn't occurred. The first was that both Terrence O'Rourke and Jerry Sadler got into the race. Without the two in the race, I most likely would have pulled most of their votes. The breakdown was: Bean-88,836; Denton-236,623; Finney-85,576; Newton-331,809; O'Rourke-142,493; Sadler-355,957. With most of their votes, that would have put me in a one-on-one race against Newton, and that was exactly what the oil giants feared.

An additional problem for me was that during a speaking engagement at Rice University in Houston, Ralph Nader was asked, at the end of his speech, "Who do you support in the Texas Railroad Commission race?" and he responded, "There is no question, the only candidate to vote for is Lane Denton." Nader has written dozens of books responsible for helping consumers and saving lives. He will go down in history as one of America's greater consumer activists. I was at a campaign stop in Abilene at the time and instead of having two or three reporters at my press conference, every television and radio station in West Texas was there, and all they wanted to talk about was Nader's endorsement. Being a strong supporter of Nader, I said nothing negative about his endorsement. I only hoped that it would not make statewide press news, but it did. It was probably Jon Newton and the oil companies that wanted to get Nader on the record, supporting me. Obviously, he was not very popular in Texas and that undoubtedly had an impact on my campaign.

The other factor that hurt my campaign was that I had retained a public relations media group out of Houston, and they did an excellent television spot for me. They also did an ad that ran in the *Texas Monthly* for a short period. The television spot was delivered about fifteen days before the election, which was great timing. We wanted it played on KLBJ Radio in Austin as well as KTBC television station. Patrick Nugent, the son-in-law of former President Lyndon Baines Johnson and the General Manager KLBJ and KTBC television, refused to run our ad. Because of KTBC's decision not to run our ad, other stations throughout the state also refused to place it on their stations. With only a week to go until the election, this was a serious blow to our campaign. They could give us no good reason why the refusal, so we could only surmise it was political reasons. The powers to be in the state all along wanted to defeat me, so they used every tool in their toolbox to get that done and one of those tools was to put pressure on media not to accept our ads.

While we were banned, Newton saturated the airwaves with his commercials. His pockets were deep, and the oil and gas industry made sure he had all the money necessary to win. We appealed our case to the FCC in Washington, DC, and they ultimately ruled in our favor. The television stations had to run our ads, but by the time the ruling was handed down, there were only a few days to the election. It became noticeably clear to us that Newton was locked into the powers to be in Austin and the lawyer for the television station,

Ed Clark (who I believe, without President Johnson's knowledge, masterminded the assassination of President John Kennedy) also represented the oil and gas industry. I was well-acquainted with lobbyist Clark and he had no respect for me and wanted to make sure I lost the race. Clark was later appointed Ambassador to Australia by Johnson.

Without a doubt, I was the best candidate in the field of seven. But when the odds are stacked against you as they were against me, it is exceedingly difficult to beat the system. Texas really needed an environmentalist and a consumer advocate on the Commission, and they did not get it. After the election, Sadler called me and invited me to have coffee. We met, and he told me he really wished I had won. I told him I had voted for him because I knew he would have been a better representative of the people's interest, more so than Newton. We both agreed that there were mistakes made and, as a result, the people's interest was, once again, sacrificed at the altar of the powerful.

Lane Denton

"Denton is by far the leading advocate of ordinary folks who have to pay the bills—called the consumer. It seems that's what the railroad commission could use a heavy dose of."

– Ralph Nader
Houston Post, 1976
(Considered by many to be the nation's outstanding consumer advocate.)

Sissy Farenthold and Lane Denton

"State Representative Lane Denton of Waco is one person who will serve on the Commission without surrendering to the oil and gas lobby. This I know because Lane Denton and I worked side by side in challenging the corruption in state government exposed in the Sharpstown Scandal."

– Sissy Farenthold
State Representative, Candidate for Governor,
Nominated for Vice President,
former President of Wells College

Lane Denton & "The Dirty Thirty"

PORTANCE OF RAILROAD COMMISSION

egulates oil and gas, transportation, bu-
, propane, pipelines, stripmining, and
ral gas utility which affects your monthly
ind electric bills.

We need **LANE DENTON**
on the Railroad Commission

"A Fighter for the People"

VOTE MAY for LANE DENTON

⊃aid by Denton For Railroad Commission, Lane Denton, Treasurer,
13131, Austin, Texas 78711

LANE DENTON'S record of public service shows he works for

* A legislator since 1971, owner of a farm-ranch, an educator administrator
* A leader of the "Dirty Thirty" reform group in 1971 in th Representatives and fought to expose corruption in town Bank Scandal
* A sponsor of new laws to open up State government to the make it more responsive to our needs and ideas
* Introduced legislation in 1975 to outlaw the "fuel adjustm used by natural gas companies to raise utility bills witl tion
* A leader in the Texas Legislature for many years in creati Commission, improving health care, helping the Texas community, and in improving services to the elderly
* A solid supporter of legislation to benefit consumers and sa natural resources, especially farm and ranch land
* Named "Outstanding Veteran Legislator" in 1973 and wa "Outstanding Service Award for Agriculture Legislatic

LANE DENTON Has a Program for the People:

* He believes in a more independent approach to regulating the industry
* Believes that the Railroad Commission should protect the p unfair and unreasonable prices by industry monopolies
* Will stand with the consumers and fight to lower any unreasc for fuel or transportation
* Will be personally involved in improving the safety of ra pipelines
* Will protect our natural resources, especially farm and ranch irreparable damage
* Wants more public scrutiny, public involvement, and public ing of the Texas Railroad Commission
* Is the one candidate who has shown he can be trusted to k for the people after the election is over

LANE DENTON
Railroad Commission   Independent D

Our official campaign handouts.

153

Lane Denton

AMERICAN INCOME LIFE INSURANCE COMPANY
POST OFFICE BOX 208 • WACO, TEXAS 76703

BERNARD RAPOPORT
PRESIDENT

Dear Friend:

Most of you who will be receiving this letter do not even live in the State of Texas, and you might well ask: Why is he bothering me about a fellow named Lane Denton running for some obscure post, such as the Railroad Commission. Well, the truth is that the railroads just take a little bit of the Railroad Commission's time; it's O I L and N A T U R A L G A S and the regulation thereof that requires most of the Commission's time.

Here are just a few of the items:

> The Railroad Commission regulates prices within the borders of the State of Texas which greatly affects the amount of natural gas and oil that companies will be willing to ship out of Texas.
>
> The Railroad Commission regulates intrastate pipelines: ownership, safety, permits.
>
> The Railroad Commission sets production of oil and gas wells: very important as to the total amount of oil and gas available. Reduction in production levels, etc. could make a very big difference as to shortages of gasoline, fuel oil, etc. Only the Railroad Commission has access to this information.
>
> The Railroad Commission regulates oil spills, pollution into Texas streams and waters. (The Commission has never filed a case against a polluter.)
>
> The Railroad Commission regulates strip mining in Texas - very important function, given this power in 1975.
>
> The Railroad Commission regulates all phases of the trucking industry.

Lane Denton is an intelligent environmentalist, he is concerned about consumers, he is neither a representative purely of business nor purely of labor, he honestly is a people's candidate. He is not one of these candidates that talks platitudinously, he gets down to basics. His record as a state legislator is one of which all Texans can be proud - yes, and all Americans, too.

Lane Denton & "The Dirty Thirty"

PAGE TWO-

When a candidate with Lane Denton's views runs for a post that relates to vested interests, such as does the Railroad Commission money for his campaign must be raised in wide appeals, such as this one I am making. I urge you to send Lane $25, $50, $100 or $1000 as quickly as you can. He is the man that can make a difference not only for Texas but for this nation. I commend him to you without reservation.

Sincerely,

Bernard Rapoport

BR/b

Bernard Rapoport in his office, helping to plan the Railroad Commission race.

I made protecting the environment a major platform in my first campaign (1970). This was our only hope to begin environmental efforts seriously, which was one reason I was willing to challenge oil and gas giants. Today, we know the consequences.

Lane Denton & "The Dirty Thirty"

A typical campaign stop in small towns in west Texas. Chuck Pollard and his band in front of our traveling bus. The group produced a record that became a "big hit."

Bob and Kay Robinson, both teachers in Seminole, Texas, were outstanding supporters. Bob was the best man at my wedding and a classmate at Baylor University.

Nader praises Denton as 'consumer asset'

BY GINA RUNNELS

"Lane Denton is the only candidate running for the Railroad Commission who is consumer oriented," Ralph Nader said at the University of Houston/Clear Lake City Monday night.

When asked if the statement was a public endorsement of Denton, Nader said that it wasn't. He explained that the Railroad Commission is important not only to the state but also to the nation, and that Denton can do "the greatest good for the greatest number."

Nader considers Denton to be a consumer asset and believes that is why the oil interests are opposing him.

The nation's foremost consumer advocate, in a press conference before a public lecture, also praised U.S. Rep. Bob Eckhardt from Houston. "Nobody influences Bob Eckhardt. You can only hope to persuade him," said Nader. "Texas can be proud of someone of his rarity."

Questioned about the presidential campaigns, he stated that "the most important issues in campaigns are not even mentioned. Campaigns depress major issues into invisibility and develop into a few which are emotional and tend to separate the people."

According to Nader, if we continue to operate under the Nixon/Ford veto mode, legislation that is consumer oriented will either be blocked by a veto or weakened by the special interest groups.

A neutral president, not veto-prone, would be more advantageous to the consumer than the present administration, he said.

There is an on-going conflict of interest in American politics, he said. Large corporations are on the selling side and the consumers are on the buying side.

In his open address Nader, who was recently ranked by U.S. News & World Report as the tenth most influential man in America, maintained that an energy hoax has been ergy and one that does not "bend to energy developers." According to Nader "solar energy produced in one day is equal to all the current oil reserves in the world."

There are, also, other sources of natural energy that can be developed, including wind and agricultural residue. He maintains that the development and use of natural energy is in conflict with the interests of established energy producers.

"There is not an energy crisis -- but a monopoly."

Then he turned his lecture to other consumer-oriented subjects of concern in this country: Nursing homes, auto safety, incarcerated children, education, communications, to name only a few.

According to Nader, "the highest return on the oil dollar is in Washington. The oil industry, like Lockheed and other big corporations, is on welfare. Energy," said Nader, "is our technological Vietnam."

Turning to the development of other forms of energy, Nader again pointed his finger at the oil industry. Solar energy, he said, is being opposed by the entrenched energy sources because, "it is not exclusively possessable.

"It is not subject to market manipulation. And the oil industry does not own to sun -- maybe later -- but not now."

He said the sun is the most natural form of energy. He used this as a springboard to encourage the audience to become involved in the consumer-oriented movement.

He pointed out that to become involved the first decision to be made is "How much time do we want to spend on our civic obligations in a week, a month or a year?" After that, he advised, pick your field of particular interest. Nader said the answer to the first question tells us how good a citizen one wants to be in a Democratic community.

He used many examples of changes brought about by a small group of active consumers. Large establishments have always thwarted citizen participation, he said. And "activists are always the aberration," according to Nader.

But involvement in the consumer movement can be a measure of a citizen's self-worth. We are constantly being pressured by our society to be complacent. However, "The more you use your rights, the stronger they become; the less you use them, the more they will atrophy," he said.

He ended his address by advising the audience that the cost of civic involvement will continue to go up. "This will be the last generation to have so much and do so little."

According to Nader, "a patriot (consumer advocate) finds out what is wrong and tries to make it right."

Lane Denton & "The Dirty Thirty"

Published And Distributed By The United Steelworkers Of America, District 37 Political And Legislative Committee, Houston, Texas

Billion-Dollar Rip-Off

Texas Consumers Mugged By Natural Gas Monopoly

If you haven't been hit by skyrocketing utility bills, then wait until the hot summer months when you turn on the air-conditioner.

For the greed of the oil-natural gas monopoly goes on unsated and uncontrolled.

Most of the electricity used by Texas consumers is generated by natural gas. A Texas Railroad Commission order permits utility companies to pass on soaring gas gouging to customers.

These "fuel adjustment" hijackings in Texas will go as high as $1.3 billion this year, it is estimated. Actually, the sky is the limit. A utility official predicts fuel bills will double again by late 1977.

To add misery to misery, the state government collects a sales tax from the victim who has been gouged — the helpless consumer.

The havoc is spreading rapidly through-out the state. A state legislator from LaGrange, John Wilson, warns: "The house is coming down; utility customers in many areas are

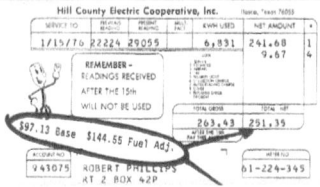

Greetings From Your Friendly Natural Gas Monopoly: **$144 Gouge On $97 Bill**

Lane Denton

Just before the final voting, I received this note from former State Senator Walter Richter, one of the most respected lobbyists in Austin.

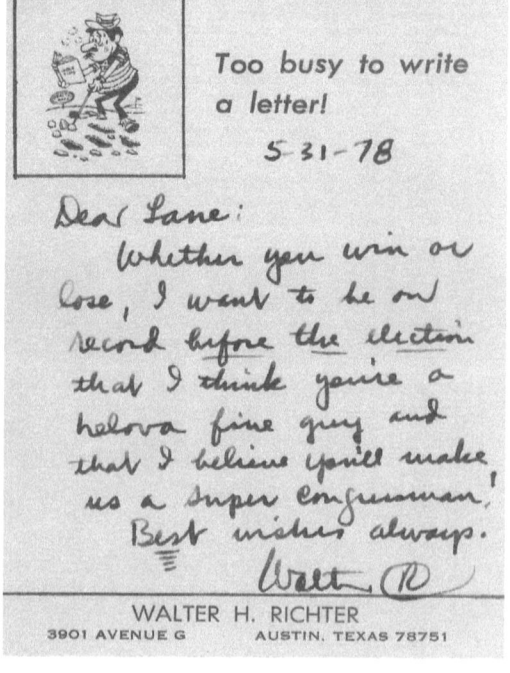

8.

After losing the race for Commission and after serious deliberation, I reached out to the Jimmy Carter for President Campaign team. I didn't take on an official position with the campaign, but only encouraged my supporters to vote for him. Texas voters had moved away from the Democratic Party. That shift began in 1964 when President Lyndon Johnson worked closely with Dr. Martin Luther King, Jr., and the Civil Rights Movement to break decades of segregation throughout the South, including Texas. However, there was still hope for Carter in the state since he could be the first Southern president in over one hundred years. I also figured that Carter could beat President Gerald Ford because the American people hadn't forgiven him for his pardon of President Richard Nixon. I was correct and Carter won the election and became the 39th President of the United States.

Soon after the election, I contacted Hamilton Jordan, who would become chief of staff, and Jody Powell, who would also become the press secretary. I let them know I would be willing to work for the Carter Administration. Carter recognized the work I had done for him in Texas, especially two years prior, with the initial meeting in Austin when only ten people showed up. He offered me a position on the National Advisory Board, overseeing all the federal action agencies. My office was in Dallas, but I did a great deal of travel, observing the operations of the Peace Corps, ACTION, VISTA, and Foster Grandparents. As a Board, we recommended that President Carter continue to support those organizations. I was also very supportive of John Lewis, the civil rights icon, to be director of ACTION agency. That position was probably his introduction into the political world on the national level. He was not working inside the government instead of working outside the change it.

Immediately after that appointment, the president asked me to head up the Medicare Financing Agency. I turned it down and the president also offered me the job of ambassador to British Honduras (now Belize). I turned down these positions because I felt I was in an excellent position to run for Congress in my district. I needed to remain close to the district. Since I had made an excellent run for Railroad Commission with good name recognition, I stayed on the Advisory Board and bide my time through 1977 while planning my run for Congress in 1978. Even if Poage did not retire, I was ready to challenge him, quite aware of how difficult it would be to defeat him.

I spent a great deal of time working with the community organizations and the senior citizens' groups within the congressional district. I became close friends with Dr. W. S. Nacol. He made his private airplane available to me and I flew all over Texas. We went to the Valley and observed all the poverty programs in South Texas. I also traveled to major cities, including Chicago, Philadelphia, Newark, and all over the South, still keeping my roots in Central Texas.

Running for a congressional seat requires a great deal of organizing and, most importantly, raising money. It would be considerably more difficult for me due to the extreme amount of territory as part of the reapportioned district in 1971. It was extended from Waco deep into West Texas to San Angelo and the neighboring counties. It was designed to accommodate a Republican or conservative candidate. I was neither, but still, I had to try. For some reason, I always ended up swimming against the tide. My odds for that seat were slim. As the time for the campaign grew closer, I resigned from the Board and officially kicked off my campaign for congress on September 14, 1977.

The *Taylor Daily Press* announced my candidacy, stating, "Calling for a return to the basics in American Government, veteran state legislator Lane Denton of Waco today became the first announced Democratic candidate for U. S. Congress in the 11th District." Earlier in the day, I had made the official announcement in Waco, Texas, and then rushed to Taylor to make the announcement there. I then held a press conference at the Taylor Airport. I was off and running in what I knew would be a wild and hectic race. It would be the first real Congressional race in Central Texas in over forty years.

There were five candidates vying for the nomination in the Democratic Party. Besides me, there was Steve Alexander, a farmer-rancher who had challenged Poage in 1976 to no avail. He had also run for governor in 1974 on a platform to legalize marijuana and prostitution, but did not make those issues a part of his race for Congress. Also, Marvin Leath, a Marlin banker and former chief of staff for Poage, announced his candidacy. He had the backing of the retiring congressman. State Representative Lyndon Olson, Jr., a three-term legislator, thanks to my support in 1972, was considered the candidate of the Waco establishment. Later in the race, Olson's actions proved just how difficult politics can be.

It was difficult enough having to run in the primary against four other candidates. I also had to counter the attacks coming from Johnny Stewart, a small businessman from Waco, running a full-page advertisement. He spent $200,000 on full-page ads in the *Waco-Temple* newspapers, tying me to the AFL-CIO and as an opponent of the Right to Work, as a supporter of gun control and as a liberal. We later found out that a very conservative and wealthy Waco construction man had funded him because we knew Stewart's only business was much too small to have that kind of money for a campaign ad.

Early on, my problems continued to mount in the Democratic Primary. The Waco newspaper endorsed Marvin Leath and the local television station, KVTX's general manager, a right-wing Republican conservative, M. A. "Buddy Bostick," was determined to stop me. Evidently, of all the Democratic candidates, he favored Olson. In a very deceptive and illegal move, he put Olson on the six o'clock news broadcast as a political commentator while he was still a member of the Texas State Legislature and a candidate for Congress. That gave him a considerable advantage over me and the other candidates. We immediately challenged his position with the station to the Federal Communications Commission in Washington, DC, for equal time and won our case. He was removed from the news program, but the damage had been done. He received considerable free advertising that helped spread his name recognition.

What is so pathetic about the Olson duplicity is that he came to me in 1972, practically begging for the Dirty Thirty's endorsement in his initial run for the Texas State Legislature. He told me he had a lot of money, at least enough to win. He also told us he wanted

Announcement for Congress. The Democratic

to be a reform candidate and supported all the issues listed on our questionnaire. We endorsed him and he won. I believed he was one of us, but that would soon turn out to be an error in judgment.

Finances have always been a major concern in all my campaigns simply because I have never been the candidate of the money people. In fact, most of the time, I was the one person they always set out to defeat. That was true in the Railroad Commission campaign and was also true in the Congressional race. I was fortunate to have men like Bernard Rapoport helping to raise funds. Ken Mueller was my treasurer. I also once again had the support of John Henry Faulk. He had supported me during my run for the Railroad Commission. John Henry had been a regular on the country western show, *Hee Haw*. In the 1950s, he became a target of Senator Joseph McCarthy. Faulk was accused of having communist leanings. An additional supporter of my campaign was J. R. Parten. He was one of the many incredible figures in Texas history and he was an anomaly. You might think of him as an unusual hybrid. The man was a successful oil billionaire and a very progressive Democrat, a combination that hardly ever existed in Texas. With the assistance of these three men, and thousands of small contributions as well as the AFL/CIO, I could remain competitive in the race.

Throughout the early months of 1978, I maintained a lead in most of the polls, with Leath running second. Olson was third and the three of us had compiled most of the votes. My endorsements came from all over the state, basically from liberal and grassroots organizations. None of the major newspapers endorsed me. My major concern was with the support that Olsen had because without him in the race, I believe I had an opportunity to win without a runoff. He probably could amass enough votes to force a runoff between Leath and me.

That particular concern became a reality when the final count was announced the night of the primary. I finished first with 38,984 votes, Leath with 29,523 and Olson had 22,929. Neither of the other candidates received more than 2,000 votes. No one received 50% of the vote, so according to Texas election law, it called for a run-off between Leath and me. Without Olson in the race, I undoubtedly would have received most of his votes and carried a majority. That did not happen, so I had to prepare for another month of campaigning and facing the need to raise at least $100,000 for the run-off.

The run-off became quite intense. The idea of a run-off was instituted to keep minorities and progressives from winning. We both had one month to win the support of the 22,929 voters that had supported Olsen. To do that, we both needed Olson's endorsement. It should have been a no-brainer because he still owed me from the 1972 endorsement I provided to him when he was seeking election to the state legislature.

Willing to take the first step, I took out an ad in the local newspapers, congratulating Olson for a well-run campaign. I attached a picture of the two of us on the floor of the House of Representatives. The Leath team jumped on that ad and accused me of trying to solicit the support of Olson's followers with the picture, and the accusation that it was a way to show how we worked together. I naturally denied the charge, but, in all honesty, we worked well together, and he was quite supportive of some of the Dirty Thirty-sponsored legislations.

We had one month to convince the voters to send one of us to Congress and we went at it with a great of alacrity. I was all over the district and even participated in a panel discussion with a candidate from a neighboring district, George W. Bush. He was totally uninformed, but managed to put on his "good old Texan cowboy" persona. During this time, I believe he was still drinking a lot and one of the issues in his campaign occurred when Bush had gone to Texas Tech and gave away free beer to the students. Ken Hance, his opponent, took that information to all the Baptist churches in West Texas. The district he was running in stretched from Lubbock to Midland and Odessa. Bush lost the race for Congress, but would go on to become governor of the state in 1994 and eventually President of the United States.

Throughout that month, I was seriously out funded, as the business community was determined that I would not win. Leath had upwards of $400,000 in his account, and I had a little over $100,000.

He also had the support of Congressman Poage and that considerably hurt my chances. During the campaign, I drove in my older GMC pickup truck, but I also owned a 1972 Mercedes Benz diesel. The Leath campaign produced a cartoon of me sitting in the Mercedes. They delivered that cartoon to every morning coffee shop throughout the district. The fact that I was sitting in that Mercedes did not go over well with many farmers and poorer constituents in the district.

However, what ultimately sealed my fate were the actions of Olson. At an appearance at the Rotary Club in Waco, he announced his support for Leath. Of all the duplicitous, back-biting attempts over the years to defeat me, I believe this one was the worst. He owed his career to me, but I guess, just like O'Rourke's betrayal in the Railroad Commissioner's race, Olson felt no obligation to acknowledge what I had done for him in the past. Olson would later be appointed ambassador to Sweden. When a group of senior citizens from the district visited Sweden, he held a reception for them. Half the seniors refused to attend. An interesting aside is that my sister, Sue Swaner did attend, she was the travel coordinator and spoke to the ambassador.

Leath won the race. It is an interesting fact that John F. Kennedy was elected to Congress with 36% of the vote and no run-off. That is the same percentage I received in 1978. That night of the election, I went over to Leath's campaign headquarters and congratulated him on the victory. He later asked that I not challenge him in the next election because he was not sure he could do it all over again with me as his competition. In January 1979, we talked by phone, and he suggested I consider taking a job as Director of the Southwest Regional Council of the Intergovernmental Affairs Office of the

White House. The position required coordination between the White House and the mayors, county judges, and governors within the 5th region of the federal government. He assured me he could get me the appointment from the Carter Administration. The job paid well, and it put me on the staff of the Intergovernmental Affairs Office of the White House. I accepted the offer and got the job and again, placing me right in the middle of the national political scene. I would not run for office again until 1982.

Departing for a fact-finding to study action agencies. Frank Sustaita and Crawford Long accompanied me and they are excellent Democrats.

Lane Denton & "The Dirty Thirty"

THE WHITE HOUSE
WASHINGTON

May 24, 1977

To Lane Denton

I appreciate your willingness to participate in the Citizen's Review Project of ACTION, and am looking forward to the final report of your findings.

The underlying philosophy of this Project is important and timely. It joins the talents of citizens from nonprofit organizations and from business together with those of government. Moreover, its major purpose is to enhance both the quality of life of communities and the efficiency and effectiveness of government.

I am confident that a new understanding of government and spirit of community will result from cooperative projects such as this.

Sincerely,

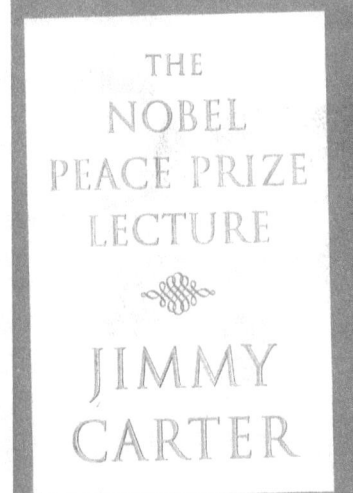

THE NOBEL PEACE PRIZE LECTURE

JIMMY CARTER

To Lane Denton —
Carter

Lane Denton

Official campaign photo

Ms. Don Purcell served on my campaign staff. She was a member of Women's Army Corp–World War II. She helped soldiers get ready for the Omaha Beach invasion. I could write a book about her experiences.

Every campaign must have someone to do bookkeeping. Ken Mueller was always available and he and his wife, Kay, were great Democrats. Wilson Abney (middle) was a legislative aide who had a distinguished career as General Counsel of the US Senate Ethics Committee.

Lane Denton

The best campaign staff ever assembled.

I am forever grateful to have worked with such talented people.

Hope Dominguez

John Thomas

David Wingard

Dewayne Beck

Bob Mullins

Steve Giles

Jack Holcomb

Connie Holloway

John DeVries

Hayward Thompson

Wilson Abney

John Henry Faulk was always available. Faulk was a great American and a Democrat.

Talking with campaign staff.

Lane Denton

A small businessman placed this full-page ad nineteen times. Evidence came out after the campaign. The money was secret and one of the first examples of dark money.

Lane Denton & "The Dirty Thirty"

Lane Denton

It seems that the trend in this decade has been for politicians to work toward the eroding of many of the advancements that we achieved in the 60's. It is, therefore, imperative that we elect someone who has a proven record that he is sensitive to the needs of our community, the poor, and the old. Lane Denton is such a man and during the three terms in the Texas Legislature, he was consistent and fair in such critical areas as government reform, health care, child care, education, rights of senior citizns, utility regulation and benefits of working men and women. Lane Denton has distinguished himself as Vice-President of the Texas Urban League. There is no other candidate in this race who has a record that will equal or surpass that of Lane Denton when it comes to working for the welfare of the common man.

The people who know Lane Denton always vote for him. In fact in our voting boxes, he has never received less than 95% of the vote and in 1974, he received 100% of the vote. We hope you will do everything in your power to see that Lane Denton carries your voting boxes.

We, the undersigned, enthusiastically endorse and support Lane Denton for United States Congress and urge you to join us in victory.

Sincerely yours,

Fred Hicks
Board Member, Texas Urban League

Mrs. Mary F. Satchell
Secretary, United Precinct Organization

Thomas W Estell
A. Phillip Randolph

J. C. Reid
Manager, Atlanta Life

Kling R. Holt
Director, Doris Miller Y.M.C.A.

Dr. E. L. Harrison
Waco I.S.D. Board Member

M. L. Cooper Jr.
President, Waco-McLennan County N.A.A.C.P.

Clarence Cline
President, A. Phillip Randolph Chapter

Ernest B. People
President, Black Political Cacus McLennan County

Robert Gilbert
Waco I.S.D. Board Member

William Odhuan
President, North Waco Neighborhood Center

Bob Kell
Board Member, East Waco Democrats

Check appropriate boxes and mail to Lane Denton, P.O. Box 3204, Waco, Texas 76707.

☐ I want to do volunteer work ☐ I want a yard sign
☐ I want to make a contribution ☐ I want a bumper sticker
☐ I will send postcards ☐ I will host a coffee

Name _____
Address _____ Town _____
Zip _____ Phone _____

I received 98% of all the Black votes in the congressional district. Every organization supported my campaign.

> Dear Mr. Denton,
> Thank you for sending the pictures.
> I helped My Mommy vote for you.
> We did not want Mr. Leath to win.
> We wanted you to win.
> Will you come visit us?
>
> Love,
>
> Jack
> and
> Matt

After the election, I received this note from Jack and Matt. This makes the long hours and hard work worthwhile.

Kennedy '80

1250 22nd Street
Washington, D.C.
202-861-6000

October 1, 1980

Mr. Lane Denton
1200 Lewis Street
Waco, TX 76705

Dear Lane:

I have many treasured memories of the 1980 campaign, but above all, I will remember how you sailed with me, sometimes against the wind, and stayed the course all the way to the convention.

You and your friends and fellow workers in the KENNEDY FOR PRESIDENT organization were the heart and soul of our campaign. Challenged in defeat, heartened in victory, we stood together, united by our cause and our commitment to an America of progress and fairness.

As I said in New York, I was blessed in this campaign with golden friends. You are one of those friends. It is because of you that "the work goes on, the cause endures, the hope still lives." It was a privilege for me to work with you.

I hope you stay in touch with me, send me your thoughts and your ideas. I look forward to hearing from you and seeing you again.

With gratitude,

Lane Denton & "The Dirty Thirty"

Talking with student campaign staff.

9.

It was not long after I took the job with the federal government that an additional opportunity came available. The Carter Administration had appointed Eddie Bernice Johnson, my colleague in the State Legislature, Regional Director for Health Education and Welfare. The headquarters for the region was in Dallas, Texas. My headquarters was also in the Earle Cabell Federal Building in Dallas, and we often crossed paths in doing our jobs.

Before her election to the state legislature, Eddie Bernice had been a registered nurse. So, her original field was health care. I raise that point because, during this same period, a position came available in Secretary Joseph Califano's Health Education Welfare (HEW) Office in Washington, DC. I felt this was a perfect position for Eddie Bernice, and I contacted Califano and suggested she be considered for that position. I had met Califano during the brief period I had worked for the administration. She got the job, moved to Washington, DC, and joined Califano's staff in a key position. Eddie Bernice went on to win a congressional seat from the 30th Congressional District in Texas in 1992. She has the very distinct honor of being the first nurse ever elected to the United States Congress.

Califano decided not to name a replacement to the regional director's position. Instead, he asked a very close friend of mine,

Thomas Higgins, the Regional Director of the 6th Region, based in Iowa, to take over responsibilities in Dallas. That additional territory was clearly too much for any one person to handle. When Tom arrived in Dallas, he asked to meet with me and asked if I would consider coming over to work for HEW. He knew I could be helpful to his mission there.

I appreciated his confidence in me and agreed to consider changing jobs, but only with one important stipulation. The Carter Administration would have to make universal health care and Medicare, to include vision and dental coverage in the next election. I was convinced that the only way Carter could get reelected was to concentrate on health issues. He was clearly working with two major negatives: 1) the taking of the hostages in Iran, and 2) an out-of-control economy with inflation escalating almost weekly. It was mandatory that the president break the cycle of high-interest rates and extremely high inflation. What worked to his advantage was that every Democratic president since Franklin Delano Roosevelt had made health care a major issue. Making health issues to key campaign strategy could possibly excite the old Democratic Party coalition and save his presidency.

Hamilton Jordan and the other strategists in the White House thought my suggestion was too much, too fast, and they chose to concentrate on the energy issue. I knew that was a losing strategy, so I turned down the offer to work with Tom and continued in my present position until a better opportunity would come along.

That finally happened in late 1979. Congressman Jim Mattox asked me to come over to the Census Bureau and work to increase the number of Hispanics and Blacks in the census numbers in Texas. Mattox believed, and rightfully so, that the Democratic Party allowed the Republicans to dominate the census reporting in Texas, always under-representing Hispanics and other minorities. That clearly gave them a distinct advantage for national and state representatives and in the distribution of resources to the various governmental districts throughout the state. I believed in what he wanted to accomplish.

I shared his goal and left my position with the intergovernmental agency for a position with the Census Bureau in the Department of Commerce. Mattox wanted me to set up a system where we could get people working in a campaign to get the count up among minorities. I worked closely with Tom Green, a Jim Mattox staffer in Dallas. Our goal was to build a statewide network of young people who would register to vote. Even though it was not apparent and could not be, we hoped that this new network of voters would vote as Democrats. Keeping Texas as a Democratic state was within striking distance and a heavy Hispanic registration was the secret to our success.

We were making great strides toward accomplishing our goal when I received an unexpected telephone call from Steve Smith, brother-in-law of Senator Ted Kennedy. The Kennedy campaign for president was gearing up for a straw vote scheduled in the state of Florida. The thinking was that if Kennedy could beat Carter in the Florida straw vote, his chances of winning the nomination from a sitting president would improve considerably. They wanted my help in Tampa, Florida. I took on the challenge. I took a leave of absence from my job with the Census Bureau and headed for Tampa.

The very short time I was there, we were doing an excellent job of lining up support for the senator. Working alongside Harold Ickes, Jr., we had put together an incredible operation. If the remainder of the state was doing as well as we were, our chance of beating Carter was quite good. And if we beat a sitting president in a straw vote, that would be enough reason for him to announce he would not seek reelection. We believed Kennedy could defeat the Republican Candidate to be, Ronald Reagan.

The straw vote occurred on October 7, the same day a major march for gay and human rights was taking place in Washington, DC. A large contingent of gay support out of Fort Lauderdale went to the march and if they had stayed in the state and voted, Kennedy would have won the straw vote.

After the straw poll, I wasn't sure what I wanted to do. I did not want to go back to the Census. I knew the Carter people would be coming after me, even though I had worked the straw poll for Kennedy. They knew just how valuable my advice could be for them in a state like Texas. As it was, I knew they would probably even lose Texas.

It turned out that Kennedy wanted me on his team. He called me soon after the straw vote and asked me to join his team. Jody Powell from Carter's team also called me. Then Steve Smith called and told me that the Kennedy people would set me up in Florida and my station of operation would be in Tampa, but I did spend some time in Palm Beach at the Kennedy compound. I accepted the job with the Kennedy team and relocated there where I had the extreme privilege of meeting Mrs. Rose Kennedy, the matriarch of the most famous political family since the Adams of the 18th and 19th centuries. I was assigned to work with Bobby Kennedy, Jr., and during the time to build up the convention, several secrets of the family were shared with me.

The most explosive Kennedy family secret shared with me had to do with Senator Kennedy's very public scandal concerning Mary Jo Kopechne and the Chappaquiddick incident. One of the workers in

Lane Denton & "The Dirty Thirty"

Rose Kennedy at her reception for her son. I had many nice visits with her.

"Thank you" reception for national campaign workers.

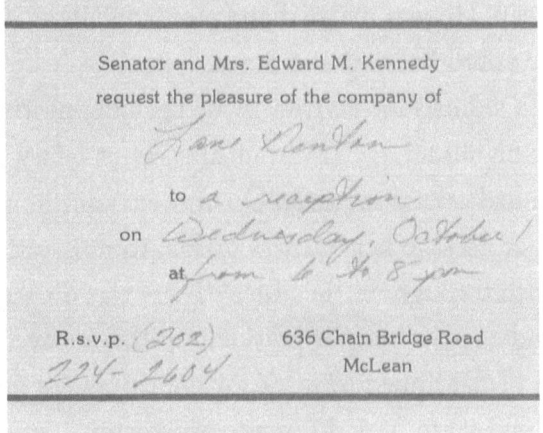

the campaign shared the story with me one night after we had gone out to dinner and had a few drinks. He described the incident in the following manner.

"Ted Kennedy had held a barbecue for Robert Kennedy's staff at Martha's Vineyard. At about 1:00 A.M., Mary Jo told the others that

189

she was quite exhaustive and was going out to sleep in the backseat of Ted Kennedy's Oldsmobile. She did and took a blanket with her from the cookout. Got in the backseat, covered her body, and went to sleep. Later that night, Kennedy left the barbecue, quite inebriated with another woman. They drove across the very narrow bridge on the island, and it was known if you did not negotiate that bridge sober, you could easily end up in the river. That is exactly what happened with Senator Kennedy. He turned the Oldsmobile over into the water and did not know Mary Jo was in the back seat, helped save the woman with him in the front seat, but she has never surfaced in any of the accounts.

"Kennedy makes it to the motel where he is staying and goes to sleep. He was married and thinking about running for president, so he could not expose himself to the affair he was about to have with the woman in the front seat. The next morning, the police show up at his motel and confront him about Mary Jo's body that had been pulled out of the river. Quickly, he comes up with the story that he tried to save her but was unable to do so. This is the story he sticks with throughout the ordeal. There was no way he could tell the truth and hope to run for president in the future."

I continued to work for the campaign and went to the national convention as a Kennedy supporter. I was assigned to work on the Rules Committee and that was quite an experience. We were negotiating public policies for the party and, of course, Carter's people had the upper hand. They continued to push a platform, concentrating on answers to the energy crisis. Despite our failure to win the nomination and the fact that the convention belonged to Carter, Kennedy stole the show with a most dynamic speech to the delegates. We all stood proud as his supporters when he took the podium and spoke out. "And someday, after this convention, long after the signs come down, the crowd stops cheering, and the band stops playing, the dream shall never die. For all those whose cares have been our concern, the work goes on, the cause endures, and the hope still lives, and the dream shall never die." Carter had won the nomination, but after his rousing speech, Kennedy had won the hearts of the entire convention.

But it was President Jimmy Carter's party, and we had no control over the platform. It ultimately led to the party's defeat in the 1980 election and the introduction of Ronald Reagan as the new president of the country. Hamilton Jordan, Jody Powell, and the other Carter campaign strategist must carry the blame for twelve years (four with George H. W. Bush and eight with Reagan) of conservative control of the country.

With the campaign over, I returned to Waco and considered my options. Did I want to run for office and do something else with my life? By early 1982, I made that decision. Once again, I would get into the horse race of politics, this time running for Texas State Treasurer.

Lane Denton

1980
Official Report of the Proceedings of the Democratic National Convention

It was an honor to serve on the DNC's Rules Committee.

Lane Denton & "The Dirty Thirty"

tion 1980

*To Lane Denton
with thanks
Ted Kennedy
1980*

CRATS IN NEW YORK

ause Endures, the Hope Still Lives'

Finally, we cannot have a fair prosperity in isolation from a fair society.

National Health Insurance

So I will continue to stand for national health insurance. We must not surrender to the relentless medical inflation that can bankrupt almost anyone—and that may soon break the budgets of government at every level.

Let us insist on real controls over what doctors and hospitals can charge. Let us resolve that the state of a family's health shall never depend on the size of a family's wealth.

The president, the vice president, and the members of Congress have a medical plan that meets their needs in full. Whenever senators and representatives catch a little cold, the Capitol physician will see them immediately, treat them promptly, and fill a prescription on the spot. We do not get a bill even if we ask for it. And when do you think was the last time a member of Congress asked for a bill from the federal government?

I say again, as I have said before: If health insurance is good enough for the president, the vice president, and the Congress of the United States, then it is good enough for all of you and for every family in America.

There were some who said we should be silent about our differences on issues during this convention. But the heritage of the Democratic Party has been a history of democracy. We fight hard because we care deeply about our principles and purpose. We did not flee this struggle. And we wel-

journey and always before us shines that ideal of liberty and justice for all.

In closing, let me say a few words to all those I have met and all those who have supported me at this convention and across the country.

You Gave Me Your Help

There were hard hours on our journey. Often we sailed against the wind, but always we kept our rudder true. There were so many of you who stayed the course and shared our hope. You gave your help; but even more you gave your hearts. Because of you this has been a happy campaign. You welcomed Joan and me and our family into your homes and neighborhoods, your churches, your campuses and your union halls. When I think back on all the miles and all the months and all the memories, I think of you. I recall the poet's words, and I say: "What golden friends I had."

Among you, my golden friends across this land, I have listened and learned.

I have listened to Kenny Dubois, a glass blower in Charleston, W. Va., who has 10 children to support, but has lost his job after 35 years, just three years short of qualifying for his pension.

I have listened to the Trachta family, who farm in Iowa and who wonder whether they can pass the good life and the good earth on to their children.

I have listened to a grandmother in East Oakland, who no longer has a phone to call her grandchildren, berent

The speech by Senator Kennedy will go down in history as one of the great political speeches.

Bobby Kennedy, Jr., and I were roommates. He should have been Democrat's choice for Attorney General or Interior Secretary. He was always out of white shirts. He still has a few of mine.

10.

In 1976, Warren G. Harding was elected Texas state treasurer. Some claimed he won the election because of his name. Even though he was not related to the former President of the United States, with the same name, it probably afforded him some advantage. Harding had first been elected County Treasurer in Dallas County and he was just a very friendly, nice man.

Because of his congenial personality, I was surprised, as were many others, when the Travis County District Attorney led an investigation that culminated in a Grand Jury indictment. The charge was so trivial, I immediately knew the entire situation was political. Evidently, his secretary had typed some "thank you" responses to his supporters on official state stationery. It was something not uncommon and other elected officials would often do the same. But it was illegal. I soon learned there was a lot more behind this indictment that certainly made it suspicious.

The Grand Jury consisted of Democratic women activists in Travis County. Close friends of Ann Richards worked behind the scenes to get Harding indicted. At the time, Ann was a county commissioner in Travis County. I had known Ann for many years, and she was considered a liberal and a reformer. It was also known that she planned to challenge Harding in the Democratic Primary for

Lane Denton

For State Treasurer
P. O. BOX 3204
WACO, TEXAS 76707

An Experienced Public Servant

Lane Denton served in the Texas Legislature for six years. He became chairman of a major House committee in 1975 and has become a national legislative leader in the fields of mental health care and problems of senior citizens

A Record of Integrity In Private and Public Life

Lane Denton is forthright, honest and thrifty. As a Baptist deacon, Lane strongly believes in honesty and hard work. His roots are in the soil and his vision is on the horizon. He is not afraid to talk about recovering

Scandal-Busting Honest Man

Lane was a leader of the coalition legislators who cleaned up state government in Texas after the Sharpstown banking scandal. Lane authored landmark "cleanup" legislation, passing our state's first major ethics, open records, financial disclosure, open meetings, and lobby control legislation.

Two Decades of Leadership

Lane Denton is no newcomer to leadership. In the late 1950s, he became a student leader in a rural high school and later taught school for eight years in McLennan County. During his legislative career, Lane was chosen the Outstanding Veteran Legislator of 1973. He has also received the Distinguished Service Award for Agriculture, Certificate of Merit from the Texas Junior College Teachers Association, and Citation of Merit from the

Lane Denton is an active businessman, owner of 100 acre farm.

Lane Denton's business experience has equipped him with management tools so needed in Treasurer's office today.

Lane Denton grew up in Axtell, in Central Texas. He graduated from Baylor University, taught school, elected to Texas Legislature and served three terms.

Lane Denton received national recognition for his legislative achievements.

He played a major role in restoring confidence to Government after Sharptown Banking scandals.

Lane Denton is married to the former Betty Kirbo and they are parents of one daughter, DeeAnn.

treasurer. Therefore, the indictment began to make sense. It appeared that the powers-to-be were clearing the field for an Ann Richards campaign.

Despite her claims of liberal credentials, but based on her record as a commissioner, I did not believe she would be a proponent for the people. Instead, would support the banking community. In fact, David Samuelson, also a member of the Travis County Commissioners Court and a friend of mine, had told me she was not a solid liberal and would not challenge the bankers. With the system obviously being rigged against Harding and the fact that Ann would not use that position to better the condition of the people, I felt compelled to jump back into the political arena. I announced my candidacy for the position at the extreme opposition of many who I considered friends. Harding also announced that he would run for reelection.

Just as it was in 1976 when I ran for Railroad Commissioner, the people also needed a strong proponent as treasurer, and I knew I was that person. In that capacity, I could tackle some of the big issues of what the banks were doing, whether they were being fair in awarding bank loans to minorities and if they were redlining in real estate loans. The most critical function of the treasurer was to serve as one of the three members on the Banking Board for the state. The board had the responsibility to award charters to individuals and in Texas, there was only one minority bank. We needed more bank charters issued to deserving minorities, and I pledged, as a campaign promise, to get that done.

Once I announced, Ann's supporters approached me and asked that I step aside. They figured Harding would falter under the weight of the indictment and, with me out of the way, it would be clear sailing for Ann. But I was not about to quit, despite the considerable odds against me, something I had grown used to in my two previous races. Ann had a war chest of money and I had only one staff person, Bruce Barrick, and only $30,000.00. Ann had received a loan of $400,000 in the last month of the campaign from an Austin developer she had assisted while as a Travis County commissioner.

She had, however, one major problem. She was a serious alcoholic, as well as a drug user. I believed that was an issue that would eventually surface and destroy her candidacy. David Samuelson, who supported my candidacy, told me that Ann had missed two months of Commission hearings. When she finally showed up, she offered no explanation for her absences. Samuelson held a press conference at the Capitol and insisted that Ann explain to the citizens of Travis County as a commissioner and to the entire state as a candidate for state treasurer why she had missed two months of Commission Court hearings.

I followed a week later with my own press conference and agreed with Samuelson that she owed the voters an explanation. Harding remained outside the fray. The press continued to push the issue with Ann until she finally faced up to the growing concern. The following week, she held her own press conference and announced that she indeed had an alcohol problem. During her absence from the County Commissioners Court, she had been receiving treatment for her condition. Her admission became a front-page, statewide story.

After the announcement, her supporters took their anger out on me. They blamed me and claimed that I had unleashed an unfair attack on Ann. It was extremely disingenuous to use her sickness as part of my campaign strategy, and Samuelson had been a part of the plan since he was supporting my candidacy. I sincerely felt sorry for Ann and pulled for her complete recovery. But that aside, it was an issue that needed to be aired. I did not actually expose her problem. Samuelson and I only asked that she explain her absence.

Following that incident and the charges leveled against me, it became an uphill battle. When the final vote count was reported, I finished third in the race, compiling 17% of the vote. No one candidate received a majority, and it called for a run-off between Harding and Richards. Evidently, the first indictment did not scare off Harding's followers. That name had magic.

I decided that would be my last run for office. Once again, I knew, no doubt, that I was the best candidate to represent the people's interest. But for the third time, I just couldn't beat the big money interest of the state. Soon after the beginning of the run-off, Harding called me and asked to meet for lunch. He wanted to talk about the race and said he would like for me to throw my support behind him. With my 17%, he would undoubtedly win the election. I agreed to meet with him at my favorite restaurant in Salado, The Stagecoach Inn, a restaurant with historical significance. It is where Sam Houston stopped after leaving the state Capitol for the last time.

The morning of the day we were scheduled to have lunch, Harding called me and, in a choked-up voice, said, "The Travis County Grand Jury has added an additional indictment against me." He went on to explain a woman had come forward and claimed that he sexually harassed her in the treasurer's office. District Attorney Ronnie Earle told him they would drop all charges against him if he agreed to drop out of the race. It was quite apparent that since the first indictment didn't get the job done, they added a second one. Two turned out to be the magic number. He took the offer, dropped out of the race, and Ann won by default. The district attorney was a friend of Ann Richards'.

My suspicions about Ann were correct. During her tenure as state treasurer, she failed to leverage state money to bring about a change in the banking community. Instead, she immediately began her plans to run for governor. Obviously, you don't advocate for major reform if you plan to run for governor.

Lane Denton & "The Dirty Thirty"

Every citizen should read this book. If I had been elected state treasurer, I would have made the book available to all citizens of Texas.

Discussing Congressman Wright Patman with Harvey Katz and Representative Ben Grant. Representative Grant is from East Texas, the home district of Congressman Patman.

Talking with Representative Ben Grant and Representative Buck Florence, two East Texas legislators about East Texas Congressman Wright Patman.

Lane Denton & "The Dirty Thirty"

Labor, Consumer Groups Blast Hike in Loan Ceiling

By LARRY BESAW
Cox News Service

AUSTIN — Spokesmen for the consumer and labor groups denounced proposed legislation raising Texas' loan interest ceiling from 10 to 12 percent Friday and accused supporters of the bill of using scare tactics to influence lawmakers and voters.

Texas Consumer Association president Jim Boyle and Texas AFL-CIO president Harry Hubbard said the proposed increase would "pour gasoline on the fires of inflation," raise the amount of interest paid by homebuyers and prove harmful to the housing industry by decreasing demand for housing.

BOYLE AND HUBBARD vowed their groups will do everything they can to block passage of Senate Bill 134 by Euless Sen. Bill Meier and a companion measure in the House by Rep. Jerry Donaldson of Gatesville. Hubbard said defeat of the bills will "rank right up near the top" of the AFL-CIO lobbying priorities.

During a State Capitol press conference, Boyle said the consumer association "opposes the needless and unsupportable attempt by the savings and loan lobby to increase interest rates on Texas home mortgages. Just as they have done in other states across the country, these lenders have culminated a massive public relations effort to justify increasing Texas' home mortgage ceiling to 12 percent," he said, adding the decision to raise interest rates "should be made by the voters at the polls and not in a smoke-filled committee room."

INTEREST PAID BY consumers to lenders increased almost 300 percent in the past 12 years and the assets of Texas savings and loan associations have tripled in the past five years, Boyle said.

"But they want more," he declared. "And so Texas consumers, already shelling out more than half their income for food and shelter, will have to pay for it, both through the effects of bigger and bigger home payments and the rampant inflation it spurs throughout the rest of the marketplace."

Hubbard said proponents of higher interest rates, who say they are necessary to make more money available to homebuyers and stave off economic disaster for the state, are attempting to "scare the people" into supporting them. "I think that you're going to see all the scare tactics in the world," he said.

According to consumer association calculations, increasing the interest rates from 10 to 12 percent would raise the amount of interest paid on a typical $50,000 home by just over $27,000 and hike monthly payments by about $75.

THE FIGURES, WHICH Boyle said are based on standard amortization schedules, show total interest paid on a $50,000 loan amortized over 30 years would be $91,605 at eight and three-quarters percent interest, $107,955.02 at 10 percent and $135,138.86 at 12 percent. Monthly payments would be $393.35 at eight and three-quarters, $438.79 at 10 percent and $514.31 at 12 percent.

Boyle indicated he believes Meier's ownership of stock in the First City Savings Association of Euless poses a conflict of interest in carrying his bill. He said ownership of such stock would "certainly affect the judgement" of anyone attempting to secure higher interest rates and it probably constitutes a conflict of interest.

Meier has previously denied such a conflict.

BOYLE ALSO SCOFFED AT arguments by Meier and other supporters that Texas money is flowing to other states with higher rates and decreasing the amount of money available in the state. "We have seen no evidence" that such is the case, he said, adding, "I don't think any responsible savings and loan president would take local money and let it go out of state."

Boyle's figures were disputed by Texas Savings and Loan League spokesman Durward Curlee, who said he "really thought the consumers association would support us in this."

Curlee said the amount of interest paid by consumers in the past 12 years has not increased by almost 300 percent. In 1967, he said, the average interest rate was seven percent and now it is 10 percent.

FURTHERMORE, HE SAID, while a 12 percent interest rate would raise the amount of interest paid on a $50,000 home by $27,000 in 30 years, the value of the home would double in 10 years if the inflation rate stays the same.

Curlee said he does not believe interest rates would automatically go to 12 percent if Meier's bill is passed. He predicted rates would level off at about 10 and three-qrs percent.

"We never asked for an interest rate increase until it was completely impossible to do business," he said.

I did everything I could to stop high interest on small loans and credit cards.

Lane Denton & "The Dirty Thirty"

NATIONAL ASSOCIATION OF FORMER DEMOCRATIC STATE LEGISLATORS

5150 BROADWAY NO. 233 ♦ SAN ANTONIO, TEXAS ♦ 78209
LANE_DENTON@GRANDECOM.NET

LANE DENTON
PRESIDENT

210.231.6222

February 2nd, 2009

President of the United States of America,
Barack H. Obama
The White House
1600 Pennsylvania Avenue NW
Washington, DC 20500

Dear President Obama,

    Urgent help is needed for the working middle class, unemployed, single mothers, students and the poor. This group voted over ninety percent Democratic last fall. *They* deserve a bailout.

I urge that immediate attention be given to the following:

- Reduce credit card rates. (29.9% is unconscionable.)
- Limit excessive fees on credit cards.
- Stop usury rates at payday loan programs, pawnshops, and check cashing programs.
- Reduce ATM charges.
- Regulate rush cards.
- Modify all home mortgages.
- Moratorium on all foreclosures.
- Immediate modification on all student loans, and extend payment periods.

    As you know, Americans owe $1,000,000,000 in credit card debt. This group cannot assist the economy by spending money until they receive assistance just as the banks.

    This assistance must be addressed as soon as possible.

Sincerely,

Lane Denton

Lane Denton, President

Every citizen should keep fighting for the poor-working middle class. I sent this letter to President Obama.

11.

In 1986, James B. Adams, Director of Texas Department of Public Safety, asked me if I would consider the position of executive director of the Texas Department of Public Safety Officer's Association. He believed I could assist him in lobbying the State Legislature since I had a record of winning battles while serving in that body. At that time, the association was poorly financed and only had a part-time secretary. With practically no resources and only a part-time worker, I took on the challenge to assist in building the association into a stronger and influential lobbying entity. Jimmie Porter, the owner of a funeral home in Mexia, Texas, helped us out financially. Porter was Adams' friend.

The troopers in Texas were below the salary level of every major state in the Union. Our first project was to get the state legislature to increase the salary of the state troopers. My first job was to find an advocate within the legislature to take on our cause. The Dirty Thirty no longer existed and so I turned to a young, energetic, newly elected legislator from West Texas. Rick Perry had come to me when I was running for Railroad Commissioner in 1976, insisting that he wanted to help me get elected. I appreciated his enthusiasm, but had no room for him on my staff in Austin. However, I did not want to discourage his willingness to assist in my efforts, so I suggested he return to West Texas and work for my campaign there. He left, and I never heard from him again until I read about his election to the House in 1984.

At the beginning of the 1987 session, I met Rick in his office and explained the condition of the state troopers and that we needed someone to assist in getting the pay raise bill passed in the legislature. As a member of the powerful Appropriations Committee, he agreed to take on the responsibility, and we got the bill passed in the House of Representatives, but it died in the Senate. We were discouraged, but still determined. Early in the 1989 session, Rick introduced the same pay increase included in the appropriations bill, and this time we got it passed in the House and the Senate. The pay raise was the largest in the history of the state troopers, an average of 35%. The Association was so pleased with my work that they gave me a substantial pay raise and extended my contract. Rick and I were politically close at the time and would become good friends on a trip we took that summer.

The two of us flew to Seattle-Tacoma, Washington, where I was making a presentation to a company seeking a contract with the Texas Department of Public Safety. Because he had assisted us in getting the state troopers' pay raises, the association paid all costs for his trip. I won the contract and the two of us celebrated.

Unfortunately, a conflict with my office secretary, Mary Pat Becnel, erupted between the two of us, and that was the beginning of my problem. She informed the Association's board of directors that Rick Perry went with me on the trip to Seattle, and it was nothing more than a gay trip. I was summoned to a meeting with the Board. Unfortunately, the Board had succumbed to the hateful prejudice of rumors, and I was terminated. I was not about to allow them to get away with it. I filed a wrongful termination lawsuit and, as expected, the Board went to District Attorney Ronnie Earle to bail them out.

Earle had the reputation of attacking public political figures for the purpose of derailing their credibility. Jim Mattox, as the state attorney general, was one of the most honest and effective public figures in the state. It was assumed that he would run for governor in 1990. There was also talk that Ann Richards, who at that time was State Treasurer, would also run for governor. Earle, an Ann Richards' supporter, was determined to block Mattox's chances. He indicted him on commercial bribery, which Mattox eventually beat, but it destroyed his chances of winning the election. Earle also went after Kay Bailey Hutchinson, who was being mentioned as a potential candidate for governor. She fought the indictment and with an outstanding legal team, Earle dropped the charges. However, it destroyed her chances of running for governor. He also destroyed the political life of the Speaker of the House of Representatives, Gib Lewis, who was indicted but pleaded out with a misdemeanor. For more detail on the conflict between Earle and me, see Chapter Six.

Of all his treachery, my case was the worse. Earle needed to find something that would challenge my credibility. He wasted very little time in starting an investigation into a contract that I had negotiated with South Coast Inc. Before all this exploded, I had gone to a friend, John Chrestia, a member of the Board, and asked if their public relations firm would assist the Association in its fundraising effort. It is important to know that Trooper Frank Holland, President of the Association, signed the contract with South Coast. During the time that South Coast was under contract, the company paid for both

Holland's and Charlie Adams', president-elect, trip to New Orleans. That also included their wives.

Earle's charges against me, supported by the two men who received special treatment from South Coast, was that I had illegally signed the contract. It was a shock to me when both Holland and Adams showed up in court in their uniforms and lied on the stand. They claimed they knew nothing about the company and did not know John Chrestia. While in uniform, they further perjured themselves, stating under oath, that they were surprised when they discovered I had contracted with South Coast. Although they knew South Coast was raising funds for the company and doing an excellent job, they still denied any knowledge of the agreement. To make matters worse, when Holland had a heart attack, John Chrestia had actually visited him in San Antonio.

It was noticeably clear to me that the contract issue was just a guise for the reason they terminated me. I sincerely believe what motivated them to take such action was their outrageous prejudice. They were totally satisfied with my work and, as mentioned earlier, rewarded me with a substantial raise. However, when Mary Pat Becnel, who really did not know the facts of my relationship with Rick Perry, told them it was a gay trip, those men, who were sworn to uphold the law, allowed their prejudice to prevail over their sworn duty as officers of the state.

Because of their treacherous behavior, I lost my case; the charges being violation of fiduciary duty. We appealed the case all the way up to the Criminal Court of Appeals and knew we had an excellent chance for the case to be sent back to the lower court. I retained one of the best appellate lawyers, David Botsford, who laid out the reasons for a reversal. However, the Republican-controlled court did not agree, and I lost my appeal.

The only consolation for me out of this entire ordeal was that the Association settled with me on my wrongful termination suit for a confidential substantial amount of money. The settlement was made after the verdict but before the Appeals Court's ruling. It was ironic that they wanted to settle because they believed there was a good chance I would win my appeal and the amount I might be awarded would have been millions of dollars higher than what they did pay. If they had waited until after the Appeals Court's ruling, chances were I would have lost in the lawsuit.

Despite the ordeal I had suffered with the Association, many of the officers still believed in my innocence and my ability to serve them. In 1991, retired Officer Les Strawn, who lived in Commanche, Texas, about sixty miles west of Waco, Texas, and had helped me when I ran for Congress, asked if I would help to establish a museum to highlight the years of service of the highway patrol troopers. It would also have a special place for the men and women who had given their lives in the line of duty. I enthusiastically accepted, and we set out to build the museum. I am proud that the museum was built and had been a success for twenty years under my leadership until the Rick Perry fiasco surfaced once again.

Somehow, the rumor of my involvement with Perry resurfaced just at the time he planned to run for president. It spread on the Internet, and he had to make sure I didn't confirm the rumor to be true by discrediting me. While I was walking with San Antonio artist, Jesse Amato, in the fall of 2011, in lower Manhattan in New York City, on our way to visit "Occupy Wall Street," I received a surprise telephone call from Mr. Butterfield with the National Enquirer. He asked if I would discuss the story that was spreading on the Internet about Rick Perry and me having a relationship. Butterfield told me that the magazine would compensate me with a $50,000 remuneration. I told him he was welcome to come to San Antonio, and we could discuss the issue.

At that time, I was aware that then-Governor Rick Perry was considering a run for the presidency and, quite naturally, could not allow me to confirm the rumor on the Internet with a story for the Enquirer. It was a known fact that the Enquirer had a strategy of buying stories and making sure they never become exposed. In other words, they were willing to buy my silence with a substantial payoff. Mr. Butterfield never came to San Antonio and what followed was a planned strategy to destroy me and, in doing so, destroy the Texas Highway Patrol Museum.

Without the agreement with the Enquirer, Rick Perry utilized the attorney general at that time, Gregg Abbott, to come after me with all the authority he had in that position. If most Texans knew exactly what he did to protect the governor, he would not have gotten elected and certainly not reelected. The attorney general of the state has enormous power and when there are no checks on him, individuals and groups are at his mercy. At the time that Abbott took action against the Texas Highway Patrol Museum, of which I had helped to start, over forty-six law enforcement associations were all conducting similar fundraising as the Highway Patrol Museum. The only museum targeted was the one where I worked. It was obvious that Abbott intended to discredit me in case I became a hindrance to Perry's attempt to run for president. His reward was Perry's support for him when he ran for governor.

One of the charges brought against the museum's board members was that they paid for the expenses of officers' spouses to go to Washington, DC, for a National Law Enforcement memorial service, and it was not a major offense for museum officials to cover the cost of wives to attend memorial services. An additional charge in the lawsuit was that I hired solicitors to raise money for the museum through telephonic solicitation, often misleading potential donors by stating they were highway patrol officers. All our fundraisers were employees of the museum. The lawsuit also included a deliberately false statement claiming the museum's "Don't Drink and Drive," program was not their creation but that of an unnamed boy scout. This was a deliberately false statement approved by the attorney general. A retired DPS safety officer conducted the program. So, the question becomes, why such a drastic attack on just one specific museum?

The answer undoubtedly was connected to Perry's plans to run for president. I, more than anyone else, held the one secret that could have ruined his chances. Abbott, as attorney general, played the role of the hitman for him. They knew it was essential that they destroy any credibility if I went public with the details of the Seattle-Tacoma trip. However, by attacking me, they also had to attack the museum, and that is the tragedy of the story. Abbott's lawsuit called for the museum to be immediately closed and, as a result, sixty-two employees, the majority of whom were young minorities, were out of work. The business account for the museum was frozen and the individual accounts for the board members and mine also were frozen. To make this even worse, the accounts were frozen on December 11, denying all the people involved any funds for the upcoming Christmas season. Personal credit cards for officers and directors of the museum were also frozen and not released until after the holidays. My credit cards were not released until May of the following year.

I consider the actions of Attorney General Abbott, on behalf of then-Governor Perry, to be one of the most egregious actions taken by any attorney general. The lawsuit carried the potential for millions of dollars in fines against each officer and board member associated with the museum. I was neither, but they included me in the lawsuit. By including me was a benefit to Perry. Attorney General Abbott effectively shut down all operations overnight and there was extraordinarily little I, or anyone, could do to stop his deceptive actions just to get at me.

In the lawsuit, Abbott was asking for millions of dollars from each board member, obviously an amount none of us had. I settled this outrageous vindictive case for $5,000. The museum's property in both Austin and San Antonio, all of which had been fully paid, was then auctioned off to a major Republican donor. Greg Abbott, on behalf of Rick Perry, did a terrible disservice to the board and sixty-two museum employees, who had worked tirelessly to create a museum honoring the men and women who had served the state and deserved to be acknowledged with a museum. Abbott's nickname throughout the capital is "Sneaky," and in this case, he lived up to that label.

Lane Denton

ASSOCIATION & MUSEUM NEWS

Museum Presents Teen Alcohol Awareness Program

April is Alcohol Awareness month and the Texas Highway Patrol Museum in San Antonio is putting on its award-winning *Cruisin' to Coffins* program. Ella Carasco, vice president of the San Antonio Chapter of Mother's Against Drunk Driving, educates teens about the perils of alcohol consumption and drunken driving through the tragic story of her daughter Alexis' death. Troopers and Bexar County sheriff's deputies donate their time to teach teens about laws and responsibility — even placing a few students in vision impairment glasses to go through mock sobriety tests.

Bexar County teens die in more alcohol-related car accidents than in any other county in the country. The *Cruisin' to Coffins* program calls upon teens to change those statistics in open discussions that address their attitudes and opinions about alcohol. With prom, graduation and summer approaching quickly, MADD and the museum seek to provide teens with the tools and the knowledge to make better, more responsible decisions.

The program will run throughout the month of April. Interested parties should contact Museum Director Todd Reavis at 1-800-795-8472.

D.C. Trip to NLEOM Dedication

THPA board members are making a special trip to Washington, D.C., for slain Trooper Terry Miller's dedication at the National Law Enforcement Officers Memorial in May. The association is also sponsoring the trip for the Miller family, so they may be present and pay homage to their loved one. The memorial dedication coincides with National Police Officers Week, following a week of special events.

Newsletter Undergoing Changes

In case you missed our last letter, the newsletter is undergoing a facelift. Now that the magazine covers association and museum news on a quarterly basis, the newsletter will only be issued biannually. In addition to the change in frequency, the design and editorial formatting will be taking on a new look. The staff hopes to produce a better newsletter for members and would appreciate any feedback you may have. When an important event comes along outside of the newsletter and magazine cycle, we will send you a letter addressing the concerns.

Capt. Ed Pringle Scholarship Applications Available Now

The Texas Highway Patrol Association 2000-2001 Captain Ed Pringle Scholarship Applications are available. The scholarship is available to the children of all state troopers who pursue higher education after earning a high school diploma. Applicants must renew each year, but may only apply for assistance for four years.

This year's essay topic is about how technological advances will impact law enforcement methods and practices over the next decade. The best two essays chosen from the submissions will receive additional scholarship funds, and may be published in Texas Highway Patrol Magazine and on the association Web site. Return applicants are required to submit a new photograph with their essay this year.

To receive an application, the trooper parent must send a written request to THPA Executive Vice-President Tim Tierney at 8906 Wall St., Suite 407, Austin, Texas 78754-4543.

Lane Denton & "The Dirty Thirty"

We are the Texas Highway Patrol Association and Texas Highway Patrol Museum, non-profit organizations representing the finest group of law enforcers in the nation: **Texas Highway Patrol officers.**

Highly trained and specialized, Texas Highway Patrol officers are on the front lines of the most critical issues facing law enforcers in the United States.

Since 1990 we've concentrated our efforts on behalf of these dedicated men and women, providing them with the finest benefits possible. We've worked with the legislature for pay increases, provided scholarships for troopers' children, dental insurance for their families, and we were there with emergency relief for the families left behind when an officer was killed. We also provide the law enforcement community with the profession's most-heralded magazine.

But we don't stop there. We're constantly improving our product and adding exciting new dimensions to the association. For example, we are now completing our greatest challenge ever: a vibrant and interactive law enforcement museum honoring the Texas Highway Patrol and the officers who have been killed in the line of duty over the years. The Texas Highway Patrol Museum is located in historic downtown San Antonio at 812 South Alamo Street, just 15 minutes from the Alamo. Your are invited to the grand opening to be held on June 6, 1998.

It is through our commitment of service to our trooper members that THPA distinguishes itself from other associations. We are the action and innovation association.

Lane Denton

WHO WE ARE
&
WHAT WE DO

DENTAL PROGRAM

THPA is concerned for the health of troopers and their families. This is why we started the **Dental Program**. Through this program, THPA will pay the dental insurance for all association members *and* their families. We want to ensure that troopers stay safe and healthy.

MEDAL OF VALOR

Every year, and only once per year, THPA bestows its highest honor on a single distinguished Texas highway patrol officer. The **Medal Of Valor** is awarded for courage, bravery and heroism displayed in the line of duty. Unique in law enforcement, medal recipients are nominated and selected by their peers.

HALL OF FAME AND MUSEUM

We have completed phase I of the Texas Highway Patrol Museum, scheduled to open June 6, 1998. A vibrant and dynamic monument to the extraordinary institution that is the Texas Highway Patrol: an institution rich with history and tradition, hope and duty, service and sacrifice. This landmark monument will chronicle the lives and times of DPS officers past and present, while honoring the troopers who have been slain while in the service of the people of Texas.

Lane Denton & "The Dirty Thirty"

LEGISLATIVE ADVOCACY

THPA is an exceptional advocacy association with the expertise that can achieve results from the legislature. The Texas Highway Patrol Association recognizes a long list of unfinished legislative business such as increased compensation, meaningful retirement benefits, and increased hazardous duty compensation. Our highway patrol officers deserve to have someone addressing their special needs when the legislature convenes in Austin. THPA is proud to do it.

BENEFIT FUND

Since the DPS was established, many officers have been killed in the line of duty. We established the Benefit Fund to give financial support to the family left behind when tragedy strikes. Should an officer be killed in the line of duty, the family left behind will receive $10,000 in immediate assistance. Several officers have been murdered since the fund was created and while we mourn the loss of these fine officers, we are thankful that we were able to help their families when they needed help the most.

SCHOLARSHIP FUND

THPA firmly believes that a better future for Texas lies in educating our children. The **Captain Ed Pringle Scholarship Fund** has been established for THPA members' children who have demonstrated exceptional scholastic abilities. Fund awards are applied directly to education tuition costs and are awarded once a year for each year the student is in school. THPA has helped scores of students with their education and is proud of our continuing commitment to our youth.

A Conclusion...

"People are not going to be silent."
–Dr. Martin Luther King, Jr., Riverside Church, 1967

Dr. Martin Luther King's comments at the Riverside Church in 1967 reflect who I have been since I first entered the state legislature in January 1971. My goal has always been to do those things that would make our state and our country a better place to live for everyone and not just the chosen elite few. As you have read in the pages of my story, sometimes I succeeded and other times I fell short. I certainly was successful as the leader of the Dirty Thirty, in exposing the treacherous and deceitful leadership in the state House of Representatives and changing the majority representation from extremely conservative to much more people-oriented. Despite my losses when I ran for Railroad Commissioner in 1976, for United States Congress in 1978, and Texas treasurer in 1982, I consider myself a winner because in each of those races I represented the best interest of the people. In our political environment, candidates like me do not win because usually when you put the best interest of the people before the money interests in this country, you will not win the campaign but will win the respect of all the citizens.

Lane Denton & "The Dirty Thirty"

Every American must begin to understand the issues facing our future and determine how they can become involved. As I travel all over the United States, people constantly ask, "What can I do? Why is my government doing the things that are not right? What is the real reason that Congress refuses to do the right thing?" Every day, ordinary people want to know why we don't have outstanding schools for all our children, free community colleges, excellent pay for teachers, a national health program, livable communities, reasonable credit card rates, national high-speed rail transportation, safe retirement homes for the elderly, free daycare, livable wages, sick and personal leave, adequate vacation time, a determined effort on climate issues, and criminal justice and police reform? The American public is confused, frustrated, and somewhat alienated from the very body of leaders they should have great confidence in and are seeking answers to all these perceived problems. The simple answer is money! Campaign contributions! Influence peddling! And more money, money, and money!

My first realization about the power of money in politics was at a coffee shop at the historic Falls Hotel in Marlin, Texas. My cousin Donald Denton worked at the hotel and invited me to sit with him and Senator Tom Connally on a cold Saturday morning. My parents, being from Falls County, were big supporters of Senator Connally. I was at the hotel to let the Senator know I wanted to help in his reelection campaign. I did not understand when he told me he had decided not to seek reelection because he had almost no campaign funds.

The most disturbing thing he said occurred when the senator told me that Texas oil executives had met with him at the same hotel, opened a suitcase full of money and they were prepared to spend whatever amount of money it took to elect an oil-friendly candidate, Attorney General Price Daniel. He obviously won and served in the Senate and as governor, always supporting the oil and gas industry.

Senator Connally was a great loss for the state and the country. He strongly believed in all nations working together and had authored the resolution calling for the establishment of the United Nations. He did not support punishment for the people of Japan or Germany. In his first race for the Senate, he had defeated an incumbent who was a member of the Ku Klux Klan, Earl Mayfield.

Today, politics at every campaign level is about money. The dominance of money was solidified when the United States Supreme Court in the *Citizens United Case* ruled corporations as individuals, with an unlimited opportunity to influence elections. As a result, the money has gotten totally out of control. For example, in the 2020 presidential campaign, almost three hundred out of the six hundred billionaires in this country contributed to Biden and Trump.

Groups and organizations also have unlimited contribution capability. This is recognized as "dark money." Any responsible citizen should recognize the corruption of money in our political system has the potential of destroying representative democracy. It is the cancer to our democratic system. Over the years, I have experienced the use of dark money through third-party involvement. Johnny Stewart, a private citizen, spent over $100,000 to defeat me in my campaign for Congress. In my race for Texas Railroad Commissioner, the oil and gas interests poured unlimited amounts of money into the coffers of my opponents. In my last campaign for treasurer, Ann Richards received approximately $400,000 to my mere $30,000.

My point is that when analyzing our political environment in the year 2022, we must consider it from the premise that money rules all aspects of the system and dictates public policy not only at the state level but also within the national arena. Voting is the essential element in a democracy. However, when you examine the history of voting in this country, it is embarrassing. I served as an election judge in the 1968 presidential race between Vice President Richard Nixon and Vice President Hubert Humphrey. That particular year, the national election was quite fair and accurate because the candidates and what they stood for dominated over the money elite in this country. However, by the 2000 presidential election, money had surpassed all other considerations and dominated local, state, and national campaigns.

Not only is money dominant in electoral politics, but it also dominates public policy. For example, in the great debate over an affordable health care act in 2009, the money interests dominated, even with a liberal president, a liberal House of Representatives, and a Democratic-controlled Senate. While Senator Bernie Sanders argued for a universal health care public policy, what was finally passed and signed into law fell short of accomplishing what he sought for all the American people. Instead, the insurance industry remained in control and was actually given a bonus with federal money, no regulations of drug prices, higher premiums, and higher co-pays and deductibles. Once again, the money industry won out. The best that the American people received was the provision in the legislation that required coverage for insurers with pre-existing conditions.

No one will disagree that every living individual has a right to live a healthy and enjoyable life, so why did we fail to get a comprehensive national health policy when 2009 was our best opportunity. One would believe that the Democratic-controlled government would have worked diligently to obtain such a policy. But our reality is those very politicians who we believe represent the people, including former President Barack Obama, are also controlled by the money interests in this country.

Public policy pertaining to public transportation is another area completely in the control of the money interests. In my race for Texas Railroad Commissioner in 1978, a group of Rice University students developed a plan to improve mass passenger rail transportation. Major cities like Houston, everybody knows, need a passenger rail system to accommodate its expanding population. When I introduced my plan developed by the students, the oil and gas giants, the automobile dealers, bankers, and Houston's daily newspapers all poured money into my opponent's campaigns. My defeat killed the possibility of implementing a plan for improved transportation for the people of Houston. The money interests won once again. The need still exists for a high-speed rail system throughout the state of Texas, and the failure to build such a system has an impact on everyday people.

On the national level, public transportation is just as deplorable. Compared to other countries, Amtrak is a relic from the past. If you want to experience first-hand the collapse and decay of inter-state travel, buy a ticket on Amtrak from Boston to Chicago and then on to San Antonio, which I did in 2016. It took an entire week for me to make the trip. If this country had high-speed train travel as other countries, it would only take no more than two days to make that same trip. But powerful money elite that controls the members of Congress as well as the president, see no need to put that kind of government money into such a project that benefits a large portion of our population.

For the four years of the Trump administration, with Betsy Devos as Secretary of Education, there has been a nonstop attack on public education. Under the guise of arguing that all children should have the opportunity of a quality education, they have pushed for school voucher programs and charter schools. The guise is a cover for their lack of concern for inner-city minorities and poor children. They support private schools that will only be able to accommodate a select number of students, leaving the majority behind in underfunded public schools and poorly paid teachers. The result is children who receive a poor education and usually will not be advocates for a change in the control that the elite has over the system, because they have not been educated with the tools to know to implement that change.

Education has been a major concern in my life. Before entering the political arena, I dedicated my time to improving the plight of young children trapped in the cycle of families having to attend underdeveloped school programs and curriculum. My mother, who taught the first grade for over thirty years, felt that every student who left the first grade should be able to read and write. But we all know that is not the case. It is in those early years that our minority and poor students fall behind, and ultimately become prime prey for our prison system. This is a convenient arrangement for those in power, who fear an educated minority that could be a threat to their power and control over those communities. However, if this country does not address the problem of under-educated boys and girls, they will eventually face these same children who will attempt to change this system, as Malcolm X exclaimed "by any means necessary."

What is happening to the environment in this country is tragic and all because of greedy industrialists. Polluted air and water are becoming an immediate threat to human life. Consistent with the race history of this country, most of the threat lies within minority communities. Recently, Flint, Michigan, with about a 60% Black population, endured a polluted water supply that was threatening the lives of men, women, and children. For many years, Flint was known as the General Motors Capital City, and for years its major plant in the city constantly poisoned the water with no regard that someday it would become a death trap for the people.

Not only is the water in this country polluted, but the air as well. Pollution in Los Angeles, California, is so devastating that one cannot see the mountains in the afternoon that are only twenty miles east of the city. From Flint, Michigan, to Los Angeles, California, and all states in between, people are suffering because the powers to be refused to take the necessary action to curtail the extremely dangerous destruction of our basic environment because it would cost them profits they are never willing to relinquish for any cause.

Food shortage continues to be a major problem in this country. The problem we confronted in Falls County with malnutrition and children not having a proper lunch is similar to what exists all over this country. The closure of public schools as a result of the COVID-19 virus exposed the problem. Children who were counting on the lunch programs at their schools could no longer receive nutritious food necessary for their healthy growth. It also exposed the problem that many children are not getting breakfast and most times dinner at their homes. This is because of the failure of this economic system to provide sufficient living expenses for all families. Under a capitalist system that allows the very few to make an inordinate amount of money, there must be the many who go without. There are over six hundred billionaires in the United States that own over 50% of all the wealth. That leaves the other 50% for over three hundred million Americans, struggling to get their piece of what is left. Since the intrusion of the COVID-19 virus in this country, 1% of the wealthiest families increased their wealth with a whopping $1.5 trillion. It is understood that capitalism needs the poor, and in this country, there is an overabundance of families that fit into that category. The direction in which this country is going, it does not appear that this flawed system will change any time in the future.

During the winter of 2021, the colossal failure of the Texas power grid system was predictable. It resulted from the reckless neglect of the state's political leaders, especially Governor Greg Abbott. Deregulation, which lead to the crisis, was pushed through the legislature by Governor George W. Bush, Lieutenant Governor Rick Perry, and Attorney General Greg Abbott. As rewards for deregulation, all three received campaign contributions in the millions from oil, gas, and pipeline utility companies. In a recent case, Governor Abbott received a $1 million campaign contribution from one oil company CEO. If the utilities, especially natural gas, had been regulated, we could divert the crisis that led to tremendous suffering and even death among the common people in the state.

When I ran for Texas Railroad Commissioner in 1978, I testified before Congress for regulating natural gas. As a result, the powerful lobbying forces of oil, gas, utilities did everything they could to defeat my candidacy.

What I have written in this chapter is only the tip of the iceberg. The problems we confront with our court system, with social justice, and all the other areas that are affected by the overwhelming influence of money in our system continue to plague our democracy. Politicians will often argue that our democratic system is excellent and can be a model for the rest of the world. I care to differ. Our democratic system is flawed and has been since the Founding Fathers signed the Constitution. That document failed to live up to the dictates of the Declaration of Independence that states all men (allow me to add) and women are created equal. The Constitutional Convention was about forty rich white men who wrote a document to protect their economic interests. One of those economic interests was to protect the institution of slavery. It failed to address the interests of the Native Americans and did not take into consideration the Mexican population. And it totally ignored the interests of women.

This country is one of the most unique experiments in the history of civilization. What makes it so unique is that it represents so many diverse races of people, religions, sexual orientations, and interests. Most countries are dominated by just one race. Not here in America. This is a country still in transition. The question is, can it handle what it is quickly becoming, and that is an over-populated country attempting to accommodate so many diverse interests, while still allowing such an unfair distribution of the resources? The question is also how long will the growing number of people living in poverty allow the few to own so much of the resources? Could that possibly be the Achilles heel for this country? Unless some extremely dramatic changes are made, as we move forward after the disastrous four years of the Trump administration, I am not confident that those changes will be made. We can always hope for a better future, but it is going to take more than an emotion. It is going to take actions by the majority of the people, to include all the diverse groups, to stand up and fight for change. I will be one of those willing to fight as I did while in the Texas state legislature when I ran for Congress, the Texas Railroad Commission, and state treasurer. Although I lost the last three races, I consider myself a winner because I took strong positions for the people and will continue to do that in the future.

Finally, let me end with a brief statement of why I entered politics. Essentially, it was to represent the people (especially children) who do not have a voice and make a difference in their future. My experience teaching in the public school system and as Director of Visiting Teacher Service discussed earlier in my story gave me a unique opportunity to understand the needs of children. Every day that I served in the state legislature, I had the opportunity to push either the "aye" or "nay" button or just vote "present." I never missed a vote because I believed every vote counted.

In my second term in the legislature, I introduced a bill to create the absolute best school financing plan that could have expanded nationwide. I lost by only two votes. I also lost by only one vote legislation that would have eliminated the incarceration of juveniles in state facilities and allowed them to participate in local community programs. These are two examples of why every vote counts. Chances are good that if every legislator who supported these two important recommendations had voted, they both probably would have passed.

Finally, I devoted major efforts to fighting poverty, obtaining nutritional programs for schools, health care for all people, and better education for all our children. I am proud of my successes, but I also realize there is a great deal more work that needs to be done to make this a better country for all our people.

Addendum

> January 13, 1993
>
> Mr. John D. Holum
> ▬▬▬▬▬▬▬▬▬
> Washington, DC 20272
>
> Dear Mr. Holum
>
> Millions of Americans are truly excited that Bill Clinton will be our next President because they have placed their hope and trust that he will be a forthright and strong President.
>
> Like millions I worked very hard for Governor Clinton. I traveled to numerous states, spent my own money, and even went door to door in New Hampshire and spoke on Governor Clinton's behalf to hostile groups in New York City. I did this because I believe Governor Clinton would be a President in the tradition of Harry Truman.
>
> I am very disturbed to read in today's New York Times that President-elect Clinton is considering deferring his executive order lifting ban on homosexuals in the armed service to the new Secretary of Defense.
>
> The new President must do exactly what he said he would do, no less. If he dodges this controversial issue, can we assume, that never again can he be taken at his word? I cannot emphasis strongly enough the importance of the new President to be a person of principles and of his word. This is what Bill Clinton is all about.
>
> I urge you to visit with President-Elect Clinton and remind him of the importance of keeping his word. If he diverts this issue to someone else, he will send a horrible signal to the American people that when pressure mounts, he will back down.
>
> Averill Harriman told me personally how President Harry Truman made these kind of decisions. President Truman would always say "I'm doing the right thing, the American people will understand in due time." I would think this is exactly the kind of Presidential courage the people hope President-Elect Clinton will have.
>
> The real issue is trust and confidence.
>
> Please do not ignore this letter
>
> Sincerely,
>
> Lane Denton
> 610 Brazos, Suite 410
> Austin, TX 78701

John D. Holum, Director of the U.S. Arms Control and Disarmament Agency during the Clinton Administration.

I met Secretary Holum when he worked for Senator George McGovern. He wrote a fifty-six-page position paper on how the defense department budget could be cut from $87.3 billion to $54.8 billion. Today, the budget is $755 billion.

One person can make a difference. Lieutenant Colonel (Retired) Christopher Hammet joined the board of SLDN (Service Legal Defense Network) and in a few years, President Barack Obama signed the law repealing "Don't ask, don't tell." The group provided legal assistance to over 10,000 military personnel.

Lane Denton & "The Dirty Thirty"

Lane Denton

"I love serving my country and I know without SLDN, I wouldn't have had a chance of staying in. I would like to take this opportunity to thank SLDN for all that you have done for me and my family."
—Shannon Emary

Friends Who Served Their Country with Distinction

Sam Rayburn
(Longest-serving Speaker of the U.S. House of Representatives)

W. Averell Harriman
(Special assistant to five presidents)
and
Pamela Harriman
(Without her fundraising in 1992, the Democrats would not have won)

Bill Clinton
(42nd President of the United States)

Lane Denton

> The Speaker's Rooms
> House of Representatives U.S.
> Washington, D.C.
>
> August 30, 1960
>
> Dear Mr. Denton:
>
> Your most gracious note of August 25, 1960 is before me. Be assured that your complimentary remarks about the speech I gave nominating Lyndon Johnson are greatly appreciated, and I am happy to enclose an autographed copy of this speech as you requested.
>
> With every good wish to you, I am
>
> Sincerely yours,
>
> *Sam Rayburn*
>
> Mr. Kenneth Lane Denton
> Route 1, Box 187
> Axtell, Texas

My political hero was Sam Rayburn, the longest-serving Speaker of the U.S. House of Representatives. I met Speaker Rayburn (called Mr. Sam) in 1960 and always helped him when he was in Waco campaigning for the Democratic ticket: John F. Kennedy and Lyndon B. Johnson.

Speaker Rayburn always called me Mr. Denton, even though I was nineteen years old. Almost every time I was with him, he urged me to come and work for him in Washington, DC.

Every candidate for office should study Sam Rayburn and learn his unique ability to make people feel comfortable, his knowledge of issues, and long hours (he always got up at 4:00 a.m.).

I felt I was the son he did not have. Robert Caro, the famous writer of books about Lyndon B. Johnson, said, "Rayburn's most painful regret was he did not have a son." Rayburn married once but divorced seven days later.

Lane Denton & "The Dirty Thirty"

SPEAKER RAYBURN'S NOMINATING SPEECH

for

SENATOR LYNDON JOHNSON
Los Angeles, California
July 13, 1960

Sam Rayburn [signature]

Mr. Chairman, My fellow Democrats:

I come to you tonight as an old friend who for nearly half a century has wanted nothing except to make your burdens a little lighter and your path a little smoother.

I am talking to you today in one of the fateful hours in the history of human freedom.

These are times of terrible trial - times of grave risk - when everything that we as free men love and treasure is threatened with extinction. All over the globe liberty is being subjected to never-ending pressure, both political and economic, by a form of Government which puts human freedom and individual dignity at the bottom of its scale of values.

We are engaged, not just in a clash of ideologies or a diplomatic contest, but we are engaged more and more each day, each week, each month, in a struggle to save the finest fruits of man's long climb upward from the darkness of the cave toward the light of civilization and human freedom.

Everything that brave, far-visioned men and women have struggled for throughout human history is at stake today. I am a realist, and I must tell you frankly that I believe the

Sam Rayburn with Lyndon Johnson and Adlai Stevenson (1956) at the LBJ Ranch.

With W. Averell Harriman at The Truman Library.

It was a unique opportunity in May 1977, when I had the privilege to spend time with Averell Harriman at The Truman Library. I was selected to take part in the Harry S. Truman Library Institute's Honorary Fellows Program.

Ambassador Averell Harriman was a walking encyclopedia of history. He served as special assistant to six presidents. He was in charge of the Marshall Plan after World War II, and candidate for President and Ambassador to Russia.

I was also acquainted with his wife, Pamela Harriman. I met Pamela in 1990 when she was raising money for the Democratic party. My friend, Bill Clinton, would not have been elected President if Pamela had not raised early money.

President Clinton selected Pamela as Ambassador to France. The last time we had a chance to talk politics was at the Ritz Hotel in Paris. My friend, Bud Robinson, had recommended the Ritz Hotel and other interesting places in Paris. Pamela had just left her workout, and she was as gracious as ever, inviting me for a drink at the Hemingway Bar. We talked about Bill Clinton, politics, and Hemingway's arrival at the Ritz bar on August 25, 1944, to celebrate the liberation of Paris.

On a sad note, Pamela died shortly before President Bill Clinton was to arrive in Paris for a state dinner at the Embassy. Paris is one of my favorite cities, especially if you love history. I always enjoyed visits to Paris with friends, Bud Robinson, Kevin Elms, Christian Brunner, and John Chrestia.

Lane Denton

Photo taken by Lane Denton, 1996.

I first met Bill Clinton, a twenty-five-year-old law student, in the summer of 1972. Bill Clinton and Taylor Branch arrived in Austin to coordinate the McGovern campaign for president.

Sissy Farenthold, Tom Moore, Jr., Curtis Graves, Paul Moreno, Carlos Truan, and I were out front, helping the campaign.

The Texas campaign had very little money. Senator Lloyd Bentsen refused to be co-chair and Dolph Briscoe, the Democratic nominee for governor, refused to appear with McGovern. I knew our task for November would be different.

Two outstanding Democrats: John White, Agriculture Commissioner, and Bob Armstrong, Land Commissioner, became co-chairs.

Only two members of Congress were helpful, Henry B. Gonzalez and Wright Patman. We had a big rally in Waco the Saturday before the election.

My congressman went to the Baylor TCU football game.

I enjoyed the enthusiasm of Bill Clinton. He was smart. When in Waco, he stayed with Betty and me and loved to tell the story of how he slept on the couch, which he did. He loved to visit with Dee Ann (two and one-half years old). Dee Ann helped raise money in both his 1992 and 1996 campaigns.

When the final analysis is made, historians will record Bill Clinton as one of the top ten presidents.

Lane Denton & "The Dirty Thirty"

THE WHITE HOUSE
WASHINGTON

January 7, 1999

Lane Denton
221 Losoya
San Antonio, Texas 78205

Dear Lane:

Thank your for your thoughtful note. I'm genuinely grateful for your advice and encouragement. Your friendship over the yea means more than you know.

All the best to you in this new year.

Sincerely,

Bill Clinton

WILLIAM JEFFERSON CLINTON

September 8, 2003

Lane Denton
Number 233
5150 Broadway
San Antonio, Texas 78209

Dear Lane:

It was great to hear from you. Thanks so much for the books you sent for my birthday. You were kind to remember how much I enjoy mystery novels -- I can't wait to read them

I hope you're well and send my best.

Sincerely,

Bill *Love old mysteries. Thanks*

With DeeAnn at The White House

Lane Denton & "The Dirty Thirty"

CLINTON
PORTRAIT OF VICTORY

Photographs by
P. F. Bentley
on assignment for TIME magazine

Prologue by Roger Rosenblatt
Epilogue by Michael Kramer

Text by Rebecca Buffum Taylor
Photo Selection by Alex Castro

To Lane Denton — Thanks for your support and all the years of friendship

Bill Clinton
4/10/07

An Epicenter Communications Book

WARNER BOOKS
A Time Warner Company

DeeAnn helped raise money for the Clinton campaign in 1992 and 1996, working with the Democratic National Committee.

Kay Mueller ran the campaign office for McGovern. Ken was my top assistant when I ran for Congress. I took this photo at the victory party in Little Rock.

This is an example of a "real person." Bill Clinton will go down in history as a genuine, likable person. I think the

Bill Clinton loved my mother's fried chicken, along with hundreds of Baptist ministers, friends, and family. She taught the first grade, played the piano on Wednesday, Sunday morning, and night. Every time I would visit with President Clinton, he asked about Fannie and Tom Denton.

Special Friends

One of the many advantages of working in public office is that you meet interesting people. Some become good friends.

I could spend a week with Merle Miller, the author of books on Lyndon B. Johnson and Harry S. Truman.

Movie star, Tab Hunter, was in Texas to purchase racehorses. I asked him to speak to the House of Representatives. He received a standing ovation. Tab Hunter was a gay Hollywood star.

Representative Kay Bailey Hutchison was always helpful in making visitors feel welcome. She served as Secretary of Transportation during the Bush Administration and Ambassador to NATO (Trump Administration).

Tab Hunter, Kay Bailey Hutchinson, Lane Denton, Merle Miller

Speaker Price Daniel, Jr., appointed me to a special committee of Texas House members to negotiate with Oklahoma House members, relating to a boundary dispute. The Oklahoma legislators challenged us to a basketball game. We won!

I met a wonderful Native American leader who provided me with a history that should disturb all Americans. The history should be taught to all students. The United States violated every treaty with Native Americans—400 total. Today, some reservations do not have running water or electricity.

Danny Sullivan, winner of the Indy 500, was very helpful in developing a safety campaign for Texas Highway Patrol Museum.

Deborah Walley and Michael Callen, movie stars who were extremely cordial and we had a good time in Santa Monica.

George Foreman's visit to the Texas House. He had recently won World's Heavyweight Boxing Championship. Note: He almost broke my hand. We had a nice visit about his favorite president, Lyndon Johnson. George Foreman is a real Texan—super nice guy.

Hank Thompson (No. 1 country-western star) was always helpful in helping to pay off campaign debts. Representative Fred Head knew that Mr. Thompson was from a small town in Waco.

Lane Denton

Washington, DC

One of the great cities in the world. However, our nation's capital has become so expensive, few can afford to visit. This issue may be impossible to solve, but it is absolutely necessary for our elected leader to solve it. Every young person in the U.S. deserves to visit their nation's capital.

I had the opportunity to live in Washington, DC, three times. My first house was two blocks from Dumbarton Oaks, the location of the international conference that led to the United Nations.

Sitting with my back to Georgetown Lacks—the canal that George Washington took to the capitol.

Lane Denton & "The Dirty Thirty"

I lived around the corner from The Griffin Market. The market had great sandwiches; my favorite, and also the favorite of John F. Kennedy when he lived in Georgetown as a senator. The market had some great photos of JFK.

I lived in the same house as Joseph Alsop, former national news columnist, who lived on Dumbarton in the sixties. Alsop hosted Jackie and John Kennedy for dinner in the same dining room where my good friend and roommate, Robert Millar (pictured), is enjoying dinner. Alsop was a close friend of the future president. Three floors above the dining room is an attic bedroom where the neighborhood story goes: the president welcomed Marilyn Monroe after his birthday party.

Lane Denton

It was always nice to have friends visit, especially Cherry Blossom days.

DeeAnn with her cousin, Hailey, Kim, and Shelley.

Hope Dominguez Reese, my legislative assistant, a volunteer in every campaign

J.L. Lyon and his family visiting the capitol. Coach Lyon was my high school civics and history teacher, high school principal, and football and basketball coach. He was an outstanding person and a role model.

Judy Francis, Baylor English teacher, with fellow teachers. Her husband, Dan, was our campaign attorney. We, unfortunately, lost Judy to cancer.

Lane Denton & "The Dirty Thirty"

One of the best places to campaign is with school children. (Note: The young man placing campaign card in his pocket to take home.)

Lane Denton

Waco students and their teacher. They worked in every campaign.
(How could a candidate lose?)

Mr. Whitaker and Mrs. Vaughn with the senior class of Axtell High
School, the school from
where I graduated. They had a lot of questions.

Nadine Baldwin, President of Waco Teachers Group. She helped with every campaign. She dressed up for visit to the capitol.

Two outstanding public officials—Jim Mattox (best attorney general in Texas history) and Betty Denton served eighteen years as a Texas House of Representative member.

"I am a part of all that I have met...
Tho much is taken, much abides...
That which we are, we are—
One equal temper of heroic hearts...
    strong in will
To strive, to seek, to find, and no to yield."

— *Alfred Tennyson*

A special thanks to good friends, who you can always count on.

More wonderful friends. They are all good Democrats

A Special Message

Sam Houston (President and Governor of Texas) made this statement about his book shortly after he escaped an assassination attempt in Waco in 1840:

> *"This book will lose me some friends. But if it lost me all and gained none, in God's name, as I am a free man, I would publish it..."*

Six powerful corporate media companies control almost all the news today. When I give talks to college students, they always ask, "Where can we get true and accurate news?" My answer: go to social media outlets and follow the following:

Jimmie Dore
Max Blumenthal
Glen Greenwald
Ben Norton
Kathy Halper
Amy Goodman
Lee Fang
Matt Tiabi
Abbie Martin

And subscribe to magazines like the Texas Observer. You will be one of the most informed people in America. Trust me.

About Frederick Williams

Professor Frederick Williams is the critically acclaimed author of four published novels: *The Nomination, Beyond Redemption, Just Loving You,* and *Fires of Greenwood: The Tulsa Riot of 1927,* and *Bayard and Martin,* co-authored with G. Sterling Zinsmeyer and Lane Denton. He has ghostwritten five autobiographies and is the editor a co-contributor of *Black is the Color of Love* anthology. He recently completed a film script, *Wipe Out: Defending Black Wall Street,* bringing to the screen the great accomplishments of Black Americans on Black Wall Street in Tulsa, Oklahoma, and the hate that destroyed it. At the University of Texas at San Antonio, he helped establish the African American Studies Minor. He taught a variety of classes to include African American Political Thought, African American Politics, a course on the Novelist of the Harlem Renaissance and African American Literature from Phyllis Wheatley to the Black Arts Movement.